The Season of Hope

A Risk Management Guide
for Youth-Serving Nonprofits

by John C. Patterson and
Barbara B. Oliver

Copyright © 2002
by the Nonprofit Risk Management Center

All rights reserved.

ISBN 1-893210-03-0

About the Nonprofit Risk Management Center

The Nonprofit Risk Management Center is dedicated to helping community-serving nonprofits conserve assets, prevent harm, and free up resources for mission-critical activities. The Center provides technical assistance on risk management, liability, and insurance matters; offers interactive risk assessment software; publishes easy-to-use written resources; designs and delivers workshops and conferences; and offers competitively priced consulting services.

The Center is an independent nonprofit organization that doesn't sell insurance or endorse specific insurance providers. For more information on the products and services available from the Center, call (202) 785-3891, or visit our Web site at www.nonprofitrisk.org.

Nonprofit Risk Management Center
1001 Connecticut Avenue, NW
Suite 410
Washington, DC 20036
(202) 785-3891
Fax: (202) 296-0349
www.nonprofitrisk.org

Staff

Sheryl Augustine, *Customer Service Representative*
Amy Michelle DeBaets, *Director of Management Information Systems*
Suzanne M. Hensell, *Director of Marketing and Education*
Melanie L. Herman, *Executive Director*
Barbara B. Oliver, *Senior Editor*
John C. Patterson, *Senior Program Director*

Acknowledgments

The Nonprofit Risk Management Center is grateful for the support of the Public Entity Risk Institute (PERI), which provided a generous grant to support the cost of publishing this book. PERI is a tax-exempt nonprofit whose mission is to serve public, private and nonprofit organizations as a dynamic, forward thinking resource for the practical enhancement of risk management. For more information on PERI, visit the organization's Web site: www.riskinstitute.org.

The Center is grateful to the following persons for their thoughtful comments and helpful suggestions on the draft of this publication:
Richard B. Berman, *Girl Scouts of the U.S.A.*
Richard Dangel, *Praesidium, Inc.*
Will Evans, *Markel Insurance Co.*
Jeffrey E. King, *OSU 4-H Youth Development*
John B. Pearson, *Big Brothers of Massachusetts Bay*

Table of Contents

Sidebars

Boxes

Checklists

Forms

Introduction

*If youth is the season of hope, it's often so only in the sense that
our elders are hopeful about us; for no age is so apt as youth to
think its emotions, partings, and resolves are the last of their kind.
Each crisis seems final, simply because it is new.*
— George Eliot [Marian Evans Cross] in *Middlemarch*

Tens of thousands of community-serving organizations center at least part
of their programs on youth. Services range from child-care programs for
infants and tots to social and fraternal organizations for teens. Included in
this wide-ranging selection of educational and recreational activities are
youth sports, youth development, scouting, mentoring, religious instruction,
and search and rescue. This wealth of experiences equips the youth of today
with the social and vocational experiences to become the adults of
tomorrow. Ideally, those of you who are leading these programs see
childhood or youth as the season of hope. It's a period when children under
your care need nurturing, while they explore, test, grow and stretch into
becoming themselves. The season seems long to the children who hungrily
grab at life, wanting to do more and more without your help. But as adults
you know that childhood disappears much too fast, and that freedom guided
within limits during the season of youth in the end can produce a hardier and
more resilient season of adulthood.

Much as the children under your care need to be protected from harm,
the organization serving them needs to be protected to survive and continue
to operate in the future. Each youth-serving program has unique risks, as well
as risks shared by other nonprofits, that should be addressed. These risks
encompass youth as service recipients, as unpaid volunteers and as paid staff.
The risks extend from early childhood to participants who may be as old as
21 years of age—older than the age of majority in most states.

Several years ago, the Nonprofit Risk Management Center published the
Child Abuse Prevention Primer for Your Organization. The single-focus book was
extremely well received, but it didn't address many of the issues about which

the Center continues to field questions. In response to the array of questions from youth-serving nonprofits, we offer *The Season of Hope: A Risk Management Guide for Youth-Serving Nonprofits,* which takes a broader focus.

Unfortunately, protecting participants in youth-serving programs is a larger task than it was when the first book was published. In *Lost Boys: Why Our Sons Turn Violent and How We Can Save Them,* James Garbarino postulates that the unspoken social contract that existed between adults and children in earlier generations has been broken. He says that as a consequence of the killings on school campuses, children realize that they can't always count on adults to protect them. Conversely, adults can no longer enter into a contract to ensure the safety of young people as they grow and develop. But you can mitigate the risks inherent in your youth-serving programs.

The Season of Hope focuses on using risk management as a tool to protect children, as much as we can, from harm irrespective of its source. Our intent is twofold: 1) to improve the safety of youth who participate in nonprofit and volunteer programs and 2) to ensure that the ability of organizations to accomplish their youth-development missions isn't impaired due to inadequate risk management planning and implementation. Several specific risk exposures common to youth-serving organizations, including child maltreatment, are discussed.

The book is written to offer assistance to youth development professionals, program managers, agency and organizational executives, board members, and paid and volunteer staff members of youth-serving organizations as they consider their risk management needs.

The first chapter introduces the concept of risk management in community-serving nonprofit organizations. Those of you familiar with the process might wish to skim the chapter as a refresher before delving into the specifics of how it applies to youth-serving organizations. For those new to risk management per se or how it's applied in the nonprofit world, you may wish to give it a more careful read.

The second chapter identifies how the normal child-development process creates risks for organizations. It also discusses the differences between children and adults pointing out the need for organizations to clearly establish boundaries for acceptable behavior in sponsored activities.

The third chapter examines parental roles as they interact with organizations serving their children. Changes in family demographics affect the ability of some organizations to deliver traditional services and, therefore, have a bearing on the risks related to serving children and youth.

The fourth chapter looks at the varieties of child maltreatment and the implications for a youth-serving organization's risk management program.

Chapter 5 approaches violence among youth from bullies, gangs and weapons. It addresses how you can recognize these threats and reduce their impact on your nonprofit's mission.

Chapter 6 examines injuries based on their source, such as poisons and falls, and from their site, such as playgrounds and camps and some measures you can take to lessen the number and severity of these injuries at your nonprofit.

Chapter 7 identifies three types of threats inherent in the newest risk management challenge to nonprofits: Internet use by children and youth. You can balance the benefits of this tool, which is becoming integral to learning, and the risks of someone turning the tool on the learners and using it to harass or abuse them.

Chapter 8 investigates physical and mental health problems that are brought into your nonprofit by young participants. Drugs and alcohol, which involve and affect both physical and mental health, are handled separately.

Chapter 1
Risk Management and Child Protection

Common sense in an uncommon degree is what the world calls wisdom.
— Samuel Taylor Coleridge

I think we risk becoming the best-informed society that has ever died of ignorance.
— Reuben Blades

For organizations that deliver services to children and youth, harm to young participants during an organization-sponsored activity can constitute a grave threat to the organization's ability to accomplish its mission. The financial, legal and public relations consequences of a serious injury or death may cripple an organization or even lead to its collapse.

Risk Is a Choice

One decision an organization must make is how much risk to accept. Avoiding all risk "just to be safe" may look like the proper course of action, but beware, the only way to avoid all risk is to close the nonprofit's doors, which defeats its purpose. A total risk-avoidance strategy would be akin to filling a swimming pool with cement.

Goals of Risk Management
- ❑ Protect participants from harm.
- ❑ Offer safe working conditions for employees and volunteers.
- ❑ Enable the organization to accomplish its mission.

Any youth-serving organization accepts a certain level of risk due to the age of the population it serves and specific protections afforded to that population under the law. The amount of required risk depends upon the mission of the organization, the nature of its services, and the characteristics of its service recipients. For instance, an organization operating a youth recreation center to provide an alternative to gang membership will accept a significantly higher level of *some* risks than a junior high school chess club will. An organization with a wilderness rock climbing and white-water rafting program for teens will have different, but *not necessarily* greater, risks than a child-care program in the inner city.

When developing the risk management plan for a youth-serving organization, risk managers need to be aware of the level of risk the organization can manage while accomplishing its mission. It's important to keep achievement of the organization's mission and mitigation of risk balanced. If overly cautious, an organization's ability to achieve its mission will be hampered; yet not being cautious enough will place the organization and its constituencies at risk of undue harm.

When children participate in an organized activity, the public expects that the organization sponsoring the activity has taken *reasonable* precautions to protect the youth from harm. The term *reasonable precautions* is key to understanding the *standard of care* expected of youth-serving organizations. When organizations don't use reasonable care, they may be found *negligent* should an unfortunate incident occur and a *service recipient* suffer harm.

Black's Law Dictionary defines negligence as "failure to use the care that a reasonable person would exercise under similar circumstances." Organizational liability may be assigned when the organization or its staff has a "duty of care" with regard to a child, breaches that duty, harm results and the harm is found to be proximately caused by the breach of duty. Unless there is harm caused by a breach of duty, the organization shouldn't be found liable for negligence in a court of law.

Legal liability, however, protects the organization and should be a secondary concern. The primary objective for risk management in youth-serving organizations is the protection of the young people participating in its programs. This is a moral — as well as a legal — obligation in many cases. Everyone behaves unwisely at times, and often no harm ensues; however, relying on luck is a totally inadequate risk management strategy, particularly when the safety — and, frequently, the lives — of children may be at stake.

Liability Terms

Duty of care — standard of behavior required in a particular circumstance. The standard is to use the level of care that a reasonably prudent person would exercise in a similar situation.

Reasonable care — the standard of care that a reasonably prudent person would exercise in a similar circumstance.

Negligence — failure to use the standard of care that a reasonably prudent person would exercise in a similar circumstance.

Service recipient — child or youth participating in the organization's programs.

Undue harm — an injury too great to be reasonable or acceptable.

What Is Risk Management?

While you won't find these definitions in an academic or insurance industry textbook on risk management, the Nonprofit Risk Management Center believes that the following phrases aptly define risk and risk management for youth-serving nonprofit organizations. *Risk* is the possible deviation from what you expect to occur. *Risk management*, therefore, is:

- ❑ a discipline for dealing with uncertainty.

- ❑ a system for making choices with respect to the populations you serve, the procedures and policies you adopt and the overall way in which you conduct the "business" of your organization.

- ❑ a framework for understanding and predicting the potential liability of a nonprofit in the event something goes wrong.

- ❑ a strategic approach to identifying exposures, including potential accidents and other losses, before they happen.

- ❑ a model for responding to unexpected events and outcomes to minimize the adverse effects of these events.

Risk Management Process Overview

Ideally risk management creates an environment where a nonprofit can take more risk, not less. The Nonprofit Risk Management Center uses the following five-step Risk Management Process.

Step 1. **Establish the context.**

The risk management process begins with identifying the role of risk within the organization. Some organizations are risk averse while others are extreme risk takers. Where the organization falls on the continuum will affect the context of its risk management program. Another consideration is how important the practice of risk management is to the organization and the level of resources it's willing to commit to the process. Ideally the board and senior management should support and encourage the use of effective risk management techniques. To establish the context for your nonprofit, it's helpful to define the relationships between the organization and its environment (the needs it meets, the legal and regulatory parameters, etc.). Another key step is identifying the organization's overall strengths and weaknesses and the opportunities and threats it faces. Consider the various factors that might support or impair your ability to manage the risks your nonprofit faces.

Step 2. **Identify risk.**

Risk identification is essentially the process of determining what can happen, why and how. In most small to mid-sized nonprofits, a committee comprising staff and volunteers undertakes this step to identify the nonprofit's risks in a brainstorming session. You can organize the brainstorming around asset categories (people, property, income and goodwill) or by departments or operational units in your organization (such as administration, finance and governance, development/fund-raising, conference/events, communications, client services and information technology).

Risk Management Process

establish the
context

monitor and
update the program

acknowledge &
identify risk

implement
risk management
techniques

evaluate
and prioritize
risk

Step 3. **Evaluate and prioritize risk.**

Not every risk facing a nonprofit is likely to materialize. Other risks may be likely, but their consequences aren't especially severe. Here is where we make sense of risk and set priorities by evaluating the likelihood of a risk materializing and its potential severity. For example, while the risk of physical abuse to a client of the organization may be extremely small, the costs — both human and financial — could be devastating if it occurred.

Step 4. **Decide how to control your risks and implement the risk management program using available tools.**

This is the most active phase of the process. The committee develops strategies to minimize the likelihood of a risk materializing and responses that will be activated should an incident occur. These strategies are then tested by the organization. An organization may decide to do nothing about low-priority risks.

The tools in the risk management process are avoidance, modification, sharing and retention.

- *Avoidance* — Avoidance eliminates risk by deciding not to offer a service or conduct an activity if the perceived risks are too great. If avoidance is the risk reduction strategy chosen by an organization, it must first determine that the activity or service isn't essential to accomplishing its mission. If the activity is essential to accomplishing its mission, the organization must either use other risk management strategies or change the mission of the organization. An example would be a youth-serving organization that decided to remove trampolines from its community-based facilities and therein avoid the risks associated with trampoline use. The organization determined that the recreational benefits from trampoline use were minimal when weighted against the risk of injury and the cost of training coaches.

- *Modification* — Modification changes the nature of risks by altering the conditions under which an activity or service is delivered. When organizations choose modification as a risk management strategy, they must first ask, "What makes this activity risky?" then, "How can it be changed to make it safer?" Modification can be as simple as training paid and volunteer staff or limiting access to hazardous areas. For example, the risk of an auto accident can jeopardize the critical assets of the nonprofit. The risks can be reduced by:

○ checking drivers' safety records and replacing unacceptable drivers;

○ training all drivers in safe driving techniques, accident procedures and reports, and proper vehicle operation;

○ conducting routine vehicle inspections and maintenance, and establishing procedures to report unsafe vehicles; and

○ documenting risk management activities.

■ *Sharing* — Sharing risk partially transfers an activity — or the consequences of a risk — to another party by contractual means. It's virtually impossible to fully transfer risk to a third party. For instance, a risk the organization almost always retains is the probable loss of reputation and damage to public confidence that accompanies injuries and deaths. Insurance is a common example of risk sharing. An insurance policy is a contract through which the organization transfers part of the financial risk to the insurance company for a set amount of money. The kind and amount of financial exposure the insurance company accepts are governed by the terms of the policy. Mutual-aid agreements with other nonprofits are a second method of risk sharing. Contractual agreements are yet a third way. They allow a nonprofit to share the responsibility for a risk with a vendor, another service provider or with a parent who signs a participant waiver agreeing not to hold the nonprofit liable in the event the child suffers an injury while participating in its programs. For example, when contracting with a bus company to transport children to day camp programs, include in the contract a provision that the bus company, through its insurer, will be responsible for harm to the children or loss to the organization arising from the use of the bus company's services. This is a hold harmless clause and should be a routine part of most service contracts.

■ *Retention* — Retaining risk is the nonprofit's acceptance of all or part of a risk, including preparing for the consequences if a risk should become a reality. Retained risks include the deductibles for insurance claims, the costs of insurance premiums and all of the risks from uninsurable losses such as fines and penalties for criminal acts and loss of public support due to negative publicity. For example, a retained risk would be the potential loss of public support if a child sexual molestation case were brought against one of a youth-serving organization's volunteers. The organization may have adequate insurance to pay the monetary damages, but could have its survival threatened by the negative publicity the case generates. To cope with this retained risk, the organization must have a crisis communication plan that permits the organization to get its side of the story to the public.

Step 5. **Monitor and update the risk management program as needed.**

Risk management is a circular process. Each of the five steps of the process is connected to the steps that precede and follow it. The team assigned to risk management in a nonprofit organization should review the techniques it has implemented on an annual basis to make any revisions that may be needed. Each year the risk management committee can also select a new set of risks on which to focus its attention.

Select the specific risk reduction strategies based on an underlying understanding of the factors creating the risk. For example, when there is an airline crash, the crash itself is viewed as an outcome of a series of events that the Federal Aviation Administration investigates to determine why the crash occurred. In a general sense, factors that contribute to risk include:

■ personnel (employees and volunteers),

■ environmental conditions,

■ activities,

■ equipment, and

■ characteristics of recipients of the organization's services.

Only by understanding the interaction of these factors and how each one contributes to the final outcome can you formulate an effective set of risk control measures.

A central risk management concept is using redundant risk reduction strategies. Put another way, organizations should consider implementing several strategies to manage risk — or address the underlying elements of risk. This ensures that if Plan A fails, there is a Plan B in place to compensate for the one that failed. For example, research demonstrates that there are four preconditions that must be present for child sexual abuse to occur. Effective reduction of the risks of child sexual abuse will involve the selection of multiple risk control strategies to address each of the four preconditions.

Another core risk management concept is the greater the potential effect of a perceived risk on an organization or its service recipients, the more extensive the risk management strategies should be to address the risks. In other words, **apply your efforts where they will do the most good.** This is only logical because the health and safety of service recipients — as well as the organization's survival — could depend upon the effectiveness of its risk management strategies.

The next chapter will review how "doing what comes naturally" can put the youth-serving organization at risk as children develop into adults.

Chapter 2
Because They Are Children

Don't laugh at a youth for his affectations;
he's only trying on one face after another
until he finds his own.
— Logan Pearsall Smith

Organizations offering services to youth from birth through 21 years of age have grown in number to meet an increasing demand for their services. Their importance in shaping the behavior and values of our youth has increased as time spent with their parents has decreased, and society has placed greater value on the participation of children in recreational, social, and community-service activities. Today, it's not uncommon for children as young as 5 or 6 years to be involved in numerous group activities on a weekly basis. Normal child development creates risks for which youth-serving organizations — no matter the type or specific services offered — *must* apply risk control strategies.

Newborn animals arrive in the world with very little knowledge. Unlike the young of other species, human infants don't appear to have genetic imprinting that ensures their survival. They are totally dependent upon the adults in their lives to clothe, shelter and nurture them as they progress through their childhood. They have no innate sense of right and wrong. They are speechless. They have no social skills. All of the skills and knowledge they will need throughout life must be learned. Yet adults place a lot of hope for the future in those young beings, and children are filled with the hope of things to come. Inherent in the behaviors that allow the child to develop are risks that could keep the child from reaching his or her potential. Balancing risk and reward is the job of an adult, especially the child's caregivers.

A child's developmental process is fairly predictable within set parameters. This means that all five-year-olds can be expected to behave in certain ways and have certain abilities within a given range. As children mature, developmental differences become more common. Physical, intellectual, emotional and social development may occur at very different rates in different individuals, yet all of the changes could be considered to be within the "normal" range.

Compare the babies in a hospital nursery with students in a fifth grade class. In the nursery, most infants are pretty much uniform in size and shape, actions and reactions, and needs; differences in these areas are barely discernible. By the time a child reaches the fifth grade, individual differences in these attributes are very apparent, and these differences will continue to broaden as the child goes through puberty.

The rates at which children develop are affected by both genetic and environmental factors and these change over time. For example, according to research first published in the April 1997 issue of the medical journal *Pediatrics*, the average age of the onset of puberty is getting earlier for girls: 9.7 years for Caucasians and 8.1 years for African-Americans. Similar decreases for boys have been documented. These changes are thought to be largely a product of better nutrition and health. There is a world of difference in the judgement and experience of an 11-year-old "woman" and a 17-year-old "woman."

Children Are Usually Predictable

Individual children may differ, but you can usually predict, at any particular developmental stage, the kinds of behavior and abilities that a child will have based on the norms for his or her age group. You can also identify the basic needs that children have predicated on their development. While some developmental variations are within the range of normalcy, other variations can signal the need for intervention. Youth-serving organizations are expected to understand these developmental processes and anticipate potential risks.

The Developmental Process

For our child development discussion, childhood is divided into several segments based upon approximate ages.

- **Early childhood** — birth to five years old

- **Middle childhood** — five to 11 years old

- **Early adolescence** — 11 to 14 years old

- **Late adolescence** — 15 to 21 years old

Keep in mind that growth and development occur as a continuous process. Children experience maturation at different rates, some more rapidly and others more slowly than the categories listed. Some developmental and learning processes are sequential — building upon the preceding steps. If the preceding steps aren't successfully completed, then subsequent steps are more difficult, if not impossible. Therefore, when selecting risk management strategies for youth-serving organizations, don't try to force children into arbitrary age-based categories, but rather anticipate their needs based upon where they are in the developmental process.

Early childhood

Early childhood spans birth to five-years-old. The most dramatic growth of a child's life occurs during its first 12 months. Infants will triple their birth weight, add almost 50 percent to their length and achieve most of their brain growth, according to *Bright Futures: Guidelines for Health Supervision of Infants, Children and Adolescents*. Because their strength and coordination will develop sequentially from head to heel, expect an infant to first gain head control and then progress to rolling over, sitting, crawling, pulling to a stand, and even walking by one year of age. Hand-eye coordination is progressing from reflexive grasping to voluntary grasp-and-release to self-feeding. To advance these important motor skills, babies need opportunities to play with toys. Risk management dictates that caregivers need to choose safe toys, ones with no small parts that might come loose and choke the child, in order to further their development at this stage.

Crying is the primary method of communication babies use to indicate discomfort. Some babies who don't feel well will cry for long periods of time and aren't comforted by feeding, diaper changes or being held. Incessant crying by infants is a common trigger for physical abuse. Some frustrated caregivers resort to shaking babies in an effort to get them to stop crying. Shaking can exacerbate the baby's discomfort, and it's dangerous and can cause lasting brain injury. Therefore, educating caregivers about why babies cry and training them in alternative ways to manage their reaction to long-term crying is proper risk management.

Early childhood is a time of experiential learning. Children have no idea of danger; therefore they explore with an insatiable appetite for learning. They learn through the use of all five of their senses. They put things in their mouths to see how they taste. When they are able, they bang things together to see if they can make a sound. Their curiosity leads them to open cupboard doors and any drawers that they can reach. Adult supervision is a critical component of toddler safety. Adult caregivers must balance the safety of the child with appropriate opportunities for the child to learn and develop a degree of independence. Preventative measures such as childproof door and cupboard latches, and electrical outlet safety plugs or covers are part of a risk management strategy.

During the first two to three years, most children learn to control their bodily functions. Caregivers often experience frustration when toilet training is delayed. Such frustrations may trigger physical and emotional child maltreatment. When caregivers overreact to lack of bladder or bowel control, they can create long-term emotional problems for the child. A child may also learn to use bodily functions to gain attention from a caregiver. Educating caregivers what to expect from their charges and how to manage skill differences will help mitigate risk.

Risk management considerations that programs for newborns through 5-years-old must take into account include:

❑ Keeping toxic substances out of reach of children.

❑ Using cribs and playpens that meet the latest child safety standards: slats no more than 2 3/8 inches apart and the mattresses that fit snugly, according to the Consumer Product Safety Commission.

❑ Eliminating soft bedding and pillows from infants' cribs, placing infants on their backs for naps on firm, flat mattresses.

❑ Prohibiting the use of physical punishment in child-care programs, especially shaking babies.

❑ Providing constant supervision of children, particularly when they are around water, e.g., the bathtub, toilet or wading pool.

❑ Maintaining the water-heater temperature at less that 120° F.

❑ Ensuring that properly installed car seats are used when transporting children.

❑ Assuring young children aren't left alone to supervise toddlers.

❑ Doing a "child's eye" safety check of the facility by getting down on the floor and checking for hazards.

❑ Securing electric wires, outlets and appliances so that they are inaccessible or protected.

❑ Securing window blind and curtain cords with tension or tie-down devices and making sure that cords aren't loose, hanging or looped.

❑ Posting emergency telephone numbers for the poison control center, emergency room, and rescue squad.

Middle childhood

During ages 5 to 11, most children begin their formal education. School becomes a focal point of their maturation. They must learn to sit still and follow instructions from a teacher. They must adjust to an environment shared with 25 or more other students with whom they must interact and sometimes compete.

Physical development is slower than in previous years, allowing time for strength and coordination to grow. During middle childhood, children enjoy physical activity, and this should be encouraged. Attention spans that are quite short at the beginning of this stage gradually lengthen.

The world of the child becomes larger during this stage. As the constant adult supervision necessary in early childhood lessens, the child gains more independence. This begins with playing in his or her own yard. By the end of this phase, independence expands to include the neighborhood and, often, routes to and from school.

Intellectually, children entering middle childhood begin to manage the abstract, but do better with the concrete. By the end of this developmental period, most children are fairly adept at handling ideas, as well as things.

Although it may happen earlier, during this phase, many children first experience organized activities outside of school. Sports programs, religious youth groups, arts programs, scouting and other youth-development organizations offer elementary school students the opportunity to participate. The keyword for youngsters in this age group is "participate," especially for those just entering the age range. For example, most six-year-olds could care less about winning a game or what the score is; they just want to play.

Middle childhood should focus on building fundamental skills. Whether it's intellectual skills or physical abilities, focusing on building skills will permit their life-long application and enjoyment. Children should be encouraged to try out a wide variety of activities and to pursue those in which they experience success and pleasure.

Socialization is a major task of this age group. Children must learn to get along with their peers and others who may be quite different from members of their own families. Corollary skills include coping with peer pressure and resolving conflicts. Adults can help teach these skills through role-playing and by discussing options.

Risk management considerations that programs for 5- to 11-year-olds must take into account include:

❑ Enforcing consistent, explicit and firm rules for safe behavior.

❑ Storing poisons, matches, electrical tools and other dangerous implements in locked, secure areas.

❑ Teaching sports' safety measures, including the use of protective gear such as helmets, pads, mouth guards or face protectors.

❑ Setting limits and establishing reasonable consequences for unacceptable behavior.

❑ Promoting positive interactions between children and their peers, as well as between children and adults.

❑ Structuring program activities to accommodate the attention span of the particular age group.

❑ Teaching age-appropriate personal safety skills.

Early adolescence

"With the exception of infancy, no time of life compresses more physical, intellectual, social, emotional, and moral development into so brief a span" as does early adolescence, according to *A Matter of Time: Risk and Opportunity in the Nonschool Hours*. "The young adolescent is simultaneously coping with the onset of puberty, progressing from the protective neighborhood elementary school to the more distant, more impersonal middle-grade school; growing taller; walking, biking, or using public transportation to travel further from home without parental supervision; and experiencing a new sense of independence."

The report continues, "Young adolescents are preparing to become adults and experiences in early adolescence help shape the kind of adults they will be. They are developing skills, habits and attitudes that will determine whether they succeed or fail in school and establish personal and career goals."

The American Academy of Child and Adolescent Psychology identifies four primary developmental areas for adolescents:

1. movement toward independence,

2. development of career interests,

3. sexuality, and

4. ethics and self-direction.

Each of these four areas has risks that accompany them for youth-serving organizations, as well as potential perils for the youths themselves.

Area 1: Movement toward independence

The drive toward independence is extremely strong for young adolescents. It may be fed by their perceptions of the degree of independence that their peers have. This drive is often responsible for friction between adolescents and their parents, and between adolescents and other "authority figures," such as teachers, coaches and youth-group leaders.

Part of becoming more independent is recognizing that parents and other adults aren't perfect. No matter how idealized their perceptions of adults were earlier in their childhood, young adolescents make it abundantly clear that they recognize the faults of adult authority figures, often going on *ad nauseam* to point them out during arguments. For example, if parents chastise their teenager for drinking alcoholic beverages, they can expect to hear from their teen about their own drinking habits.

The fear of losing independence frequently inhibits adolescents from seeking adult help when confronting a problem. Not only are they afraid that their freedom will be curtailed, they also don't want to hear the "I told you so" that often accompanies parental, as well as other adult, assistance.

Young people in this developmental stage often look for non-threatening adult mentors from whom to seek guidance and counsel. Such individuals are often popular schoolteachers, youth-group leaders or adults with whom they have formed a bond of mutual respect and friendship.

During this period, young teens struggle to develop a sense of identity. Part of the identity they seek is with their peer group. The peer group influences interests and clothing styles. When adolescents perceive themselves as not being accepted by their peers, they may resort to forming anti-social groups to help define their sense of "self." According to James Garbarino in *Lost Boys*, "Having some identity in relation to peers is so important to most children and youth that even a negative definition of self is better than nothing at all."

Young adolescents can be very self-centered. They are very concerned about their appearance and want to be perceived as being pretty or handsome. They want to be liked by their peers. They are prone to sudden mood shifts. They may perceive minor events to be catastrophic. Depression and suicide are serious risks for young adolescents and will be discussed in more detail in Chapter 8: Physical and Mental Health

Area 2: Development of career interests

These 11- to 14-year-olds realize that they have to make decisions about their futures; but they aren't ready to commit to a specific career field. They are apt to view part-time employment as a way to earn money and be more independent. First jobs might be babysitting or doing chores for neighbors.

While on-the-job learning is important, adults shouldn't permit a young person's job responsibilities to interfere with academic or vocational education.

Many young adolescents participate in volunteer activities. These activities are an important means for learning about the world of work in general, and specifically what it might be like to pursue a career related to their volunteer activities. Many schools are requiring community service in order to graduate.

Employers of young adolescents must be mindful that federal, state and local labor regulations limit the hours and kinds of employment that youth are permitted to engage in. Whether employees or volunteers, adolescents' on-the-job success depends on the training and supervision provided by their employers.

Area 3: Sexuality

During adolescence, boys and girls become young men and women and must learn to cope with their newly awakened sexuality — a process that is smoother for some than others. Periods of shyness, blushing, and modesty occur as they become used to their new appearances. They worry about being normal. Thus while they may experiment sexually with same-sex peers, movement toward heterosexuality, with fears of homosexuality, is common, according to the American Academy of Child and Adolescent Psychiatry.

Socially, they focus their attention on same-sex friends and group activities. One-on-one dating is fairly rare during this stage. However, girls, who develop physically sooner than boys, may establish social or dating relationships with boys a year or two older than they are.

Adults need to be available to answer questions and offer guidance during this phase. Observing young adolescents as they develop social skills responsive to their hormonal changes can be almost painful for adults. To adults, adolescent attempts to establish relationships often appear humorous. Sensitive adults, however, think back to when they were going through the same process of development, and will only chuckle to themselves.

Area 4: Ethics and self-direction

Early adolescence is a time of experimentation, and of rule and limit testing. As they try "adult experiences," they indulge in considerable risk taking. Young adolescents are prone to experiment with cigarettes, and marijuana, alcohol and other drugs. They perceive these activities as expressions of their independence and things that their friends are doing. They may rationalize that if it's OK for adults to smoke and drink, it should be OK for them, too.

Young adolescents don't fully appreciate cause-and-effect relationships. They tend to act without consideration of possible consequences. For example, they may think that setting up a meeting with someone they meet through the Internet is an acceptable expansion of their social life without considering that the person with whom they will be meeting may well be someone who could do them great harm.

Peers influence the moral choices that young adolescents make. When friends and associates are involved in delinquent activities, individuals who would never engage alone in such activities are prone to go along with the group. Studies by the U.S. Department of Health and Human Services show that the best indicator of whether a teen will smoke is whether his or her best friend does.

Risk management considerations that programs for 11- to 14-year-olds must take into account include:

- ❏ Developing skills in conflict resolution, negotiation and anger management.

- ❏ Teaching age-appropriate personal safety skills.

- ❏ Avoiding promises of confidentiality for information shared by adolescents that clearly needs to be communicated to their parents or the authorities.

- ❏ Stressing the use of protective sports gear and automobile seat belts, and adhering to safety procedures.

- ❏ Establishing a zero-tolerance policy for possession of weapons, alcohol and drugs in any organizational program.

- ❏ Setting up communication with parents about scheduled activities and their children's participation.

- ❏ Encouraging social relationships between young men and women based upon mutual respect of personal boundaries.

- ❏ Involving young people in the creation of "Codes of Conduct" and other rules so adolescents can feel somewhat empowered and responsible for their own behavior.

- ❏ Monitoring adolescent's behavior and intervening when it places them or others in potentially dangerous situations.

Late adolescence

Ages 15 to 21 years, called late adolescence, is the final stage of transition from childhood to adulthood. Legally and developmentally, in our culture the 18th and 21st birthdays are milestones. You expect that individuals will be capable of assuming most adult responsibilities by age 18 and all of the responsibilities of mature adults by 21 years of age. Many legal responsibilities of youth-serving organizations will be substantially different for those younger than 18 than for those who are 18 and older.

Area 1: Movement toward independence

Conflicts between parents and teens are common during the early part of late adolescence as they pursue greater independence. By the end of the period, most adolescents and their parents have been able to redefine their relationships. But programs that serve this age group still need to establish communication with parents and encourage parental involvement.

The automobile driver's permit (license) shines as a major symbol of having made it for most adolescents. Being able to drive is a true symbol of adolescent independence. Cars serve as status symbols and social catalysts. No longer do they have to depend on parents chauffeuring them to activities or on dates. Gaining access to a vehicle — especially one's own — represents both a giant step toward freedom, and a significant cause of death and injury among teenagers.

Leaving one's parents' home is another giant step. For many, this transition occurs after graduation from high school when the older adolescent either pursues a full-time vocation or goes on to college. For some, leaving home is an act of defiance — chafing against parental control and asserting one's independence. In other cases, parents force their adolescent children to leave home when the children refuse to comply with parental demands.

Some older adolescents who run away or who are forced out of their parents' homes are capable of independent living while others need either temporary or long-term residential care. Many teenagers who don't have skills for independent living and don't find needed services are forced into sexually exploitive relationships, such as prostitution, in order to survive on the streets.

Area 2: Development of career interests

Earning one's own money is another step toward independence. Teens account for a large share of the discretionary spending in today's economy. By the time that adolescents enter high school, it isn't unusual for them to hold a part-time job — moving from odd jobs for neighbors to formal employment. These jobs often provide opportunities to earn money, but not necessarily in fields that constitute potential career interests. Experiencing the discipline required for holding a job and meeting the expectations of employers is an important developmental step — but one that must be viewed in the context of other, competing responsibilities, such as school.

Adolescents are still forming work habits. They need supervision to ensure that they are performing the responsibilities of their employment and that they are doing so safely. For example, a teenager employed as a lifeguard at the community swimming pool needs to be clear that talking to friends, flirting with patrons or posing aren't acceptable on-the-job behaviors because they make it impossible for a lifeguard's full attention to focus on monitoring the swimming pool.

Older adolescents realize that very soon they will be facing decisions about their future. They need to make choices and decide if they will pursue a career field requiring additional formal education or if they will enter the world of work immediately after high school. Career paths can be another source of conflict between parents and child, such as when the parents want their child to be a physician and their child wants to be a mechanic or a forest ranger.

Staff members of youth-serving organizations are often brought into parent-child conflicts when the young person seeks allies for his or her point of view. Rather than being an advocate for a particular viewpoint, staff members should consider serving as a sounding board and offering alternatives that help to clarify positions. Even well-meaning staff members can expose the organization to potential lawsuits by exceeding their professional qualifications and attempting to offer guidance and counseling.

Area 3: Sexuality

According to 1995 "Youth Risk Behavior Surveillance — United States, 193" published in *Morbidity and Mortality Weekly Report* (Volume 44, Number SS-1) by the Centers for Disease Control, sexual intercourse by adolescents isn't an unusual occurrence. For female students prevalence rates increased from 31.6 percent in the ninth grade to 66.3 percent in the twelfth grade. For male students, prevalence increased from 43.5 percent in the ninth grade to 70.2 percent in the twelfth grade. Only about 25 percent of ninth grade students reported being "currently sexually active" compared with more than 50 percent of the twelfth graders. The same report documents the risks of unplanned pregnancy and sexually transmitted diseases to which young people expose themselves as they quest to separate from their parents and become their own selves.

Young adolescents engage in frequently changing relationships as they refine their social skills. "Hanging out" in groups gradually segues to pairing up. Older adolescents may date several individuals, but usually do so one at a time. This testing is all part of the learning process leading to the establishment of long-term adult relationships. During this phase, most young people begin to focus their attention on specific partners. These relationships can create conflicts with parents and cause problems that infiltrate the organizations in which the partners participate.

Area 4: Ethics and self-direction

By the end of adolescence, individuals should have a pretty good idea of who they are and what they stand for apart from their peer group. Peer groups, however, still play a role in risk-taking behavior. Consider, for example, fraternity keg parties, dares, rivalry and competition.

Risk management considerations that programs for 15- to 21-year-olds must take into account include:

❑ Establishing a zero-tolerance policy for possession of weapons, alcohol and drugs in any organizational program.

❑ Establishing clear guidelines for social relationships between participants during organizational activities.

❑ Monitoring conduct and intervening when adolescents' behavior places them or others in potentially dangerous situations.

❑ Clearly placing limits on decisions that require judgement and that could have serious consequences.

❑ Maintaining contact with parents of underage teens (usually those younger than 18 years of age).

❑ Prohibiting sexual relationships between adult caregivers (including young adults) and program participants.

Children with disabilities

Youth-serving organizations should recognize specific risks created by particular disabilities. Organizations also should understand that, while the developmental process may be influenced by disabilities, children with disabilities go through similar physical, emotional and intellectual development as their peers.

For some risks, such as the risk of sexual abuse, children with disabilities are more vulnerable than children without disabilities. Dick Sobsey in his book *Violence and Abuse in the Lives of People with Disabilities: The End of Silent Acceptance* points out that children with disabilities are twice as likely to be sexually molested. He also says that individuals who are part of the system designed to assist disabled individuals perpetrate half of that molestation. Thus, organizations need to exercise extreme caution when selecting personnel to serve children with disabilities and to apply additional risk-reduction strategies, such as increased staff supervision and monitoring.

Depending on the severity of their physical disabilities, children may have increased physical-injury risks due to inappropriate handling, such as when given assistance in and out of wheelchairs, or inadequate accessibility provisions.

Normal Behavior May Be Troublesome

As our society increasingly seeks legal remedies for many of its ills, organizations tend to react to some kinds of normal child behavior in a legalistic manner. For example, not too long ago media reports told of a six-year-old boy who was expelled from school for sexual harassment. He had kissed a girl on the cheek at recess. In today's climate, you can understand why a school district wouldn't want this kind of behavior from its students. Even if the media story wasn't complete, given the age of the transgressor, society questions the characterization of a single episode of this behavior as sexual harassment and expulsion as an appropriate initial response.

Gail Ryan suggests a more constructive approach in *Juvenile Sexual Offending*. She advises, first confront the child and label the specific inappropriate behavior, reacting to it on a personal level. For example, in the case of the six-year-old kisser, the first step is to tell the boy that you saw or heard that he kissed Mary during recess. That labels the behavior. After labeling the behavior, you give your reaction to the behavior, for example,

> ## Responding to a Child's Behavior
>
> 1. Label the behavior and give your reaction to it.
> 2. Monitor the behavior and, if repeated,
> 3. Confront the child and prohibit the behavior.

"Mary did not want you to kiss her and I am uncomfortable with you kissing anyone who doesn't want to be kissed." If the behavior continues or is repeated, the next step would be to confront the offender and prohibit further offending behaviors. Ryan states, "By putting the emphasis of the first response on communication and empathy and reserving the prohibition for the second response learning is possible, which has been unlikely in repressive/suppressive reactions."

Monitoring the behavior is also important. While monitoring the behavior, you can suggest alternative ways to communicate feelings. In this case, for example, you might ask the child, "What were you trying to tell Mary when you kissed her?" Assuming that the answer to this question is something like, "I like Mary," a follow-up question could be "What are some other ways you could let Mary know you like her?" Of course there may be other less benign reasons for kissing Mary, such as "Joey dared me to." That response also needs to be addressed in terms of doing things that other people dare him to do. But, the underlying process would be the same: First label and react to the behavior; monitor and, if repeated, confront and prohibit.

Children Aren't Small Adults

Before leaving the topic of children, it's important to remember that children aren't small adults. Often, one hears adults talking about the children's behavior being immature. You must place children's behavior in context. A 16-year-old acting as an eight-year-old is being immature; a 16-year-old behaving as a 16-year-old is showing age-appropriate behavior. By understanding the context of the behavior, the professional will be in a better position to apply more appropriate risk management practices to the program.

On the other hand, the organization, by understanding the developmental stages of the children it serves, can anticipate and develop strategies to manage the risks created by the normal maturation and development of children, whether they are recipients of service, volunteers or employees.

The next chapter looks at the importance of involving parents in your youth-serving organization. Parents educated about the rules, expectations and services of your program(s), are more likely to talk over issues as they arise and less likely to run to their attorney to remedy a situation.

Chapter 3
Parental Partners in Risk Management

Children are natural mimics; they act like their parents in
spite of every effort to teach them good manners.
— author unknown

Parents are hopeful about youth. They hope their children will have a better life than they had. Some hope their children will fulfill their own unfulfilled hopes and dreams. They are carriers of the family's genes and surname. Children are fresh and new. They are spring to their parents' summer and to their grandparents' autumn. Although, parents aren't the only influence in the lives of children, they are the most important early influence. From the moment of birth, or possibly conception, parents shape their children's perceptions. Parental attitudes form the basis for a child's self-image, views of other people, and "family" values. The child who enters your program is a little bundle of all those parental influences.

Youth-serving programs have to relate to parents. Many organizations rely upon parents to volunteer and actually staff the programs in which their children participate. Other organizations see the parents in passing as they drop off or pick up their children. In whatever manner parents relate to organizations, it's important that parents be made a part of the risk management process — partners in protecting children from harm.

Ward and June Cleaver Only Existed on TV

Being a parent is a very complex undertaking, and while many people do it well, others are ill suited for their parental roles. There are no perfect parents except on television. Even people skilled at parenting may, at times, have unreal expectations for their children, force their children into activities that don't interest them, or be overly protective. Parents may be nurturing or abusive. They may be actively involved in their children's activities or they may be too busy with their own careers or other interests to participate.

Staff members of children's organizations may perceive parents as being unreasonable, insensitive and very demanding. Some parents may be all but invisible to the programs in which their children are participants. A common complaint of many youth-serving programs is that parents perceive them as cheap baby-sitting services to the detriment of their child-development purposes. The organization should decide what kinds of parental involvement are necessary to accomplish its mission. The next step is to assess how the organization approaches parents and re-evaluate if there is a better method to garner the levels of parental participation required. When a child is accepted into its programs, the organization needs to clearly communicate to the parents what the program will require of them.

Critical Communication for Parents

❑ What is the organization's mission and program?

❑ What is expected of the child (attendance, behavior, participation etc.)?

❑ What is expected of the parent (time, financial support, transportation, promptness, etc.)?

❑ Who should be contacted in an emergency? How?

❑ What are the program's hours of operation?

❑ What are the policies of the program (tardiness, sickness, sexual abuse, etc.)?

Family Demographics Impact Your Programs

The make-up of the typical American family has changed significantly during the last 50 years. Single parents, blended families and working mothers have pushed out Mom/Dad/two kids and a dog as the norm and created demands for additional services for children — especially child-care programs. The changing family demographics have also shrunk the traditional pool of volunteers available for daytime and after-school programs.

The most significant change has been a 68 percent increase in the number of two-income families. According to the U.S. Bureau of the Census, in 1998 there were more than 26 million married couples with children under 18 who were both employed. When both parents work, child care shifts to other caregivers, and parents have less free time to volunteer their time and skills.

The number of single-parent families has also increased. In 1998, 30 percent of U.S. families with children younger than 18 were headed by a single parent, reports the U.S. Census Bureau. Of these families, single mothers headed more than 80 percent. When single mothers head families, those families are much more likely to subsist at below poverty levels than when headed by two parents or even by a single father.

These shifts in family demographics have forced changes in the way that some organizations function. Demographic changes have also created demands for new child-care services. For example, many activities for middle childhood youngsters that traditionally had been held after school have been moved to early evenings or weekends. Organizations that in the past accepted only male volunteers for some positions have diversified their volunteer pool and are actively seeking to involve single mothers. Some organizations serving wealthier families have forsaken volunteers entirely and hired part-time, youth-group leaders and coaches. The improved health and longevity of senior citizens, has encouraged some organizations to recruit grandparents to fill roles that traditionally had been reserved for parents.

Parents Aren't the Enemy

Invariably, youth-serving organizations will need parental involvement — in fact, strong organizations look for creative ways to involve parents. To be successful, parental involvement requires educating parents about the organization's expectations for them and for their children.

Explain the parameters of the organization's program to parents.

Chances are mothers won't know a lot about Boy Scouts or other male-only programs, just as fathers won't know a lot about Girl Scouts or other programs for their daughters. Rather than assume that parents are knowledgeable, organizations need to provide them with educational materials and an orientation. Assumptions can backfire. The mother of a child injured during a program-sponsored activity sued the organization, stating that if she had been aware that the program included that activity, she wouldn't have allowed her son to participate.

Provide ongoing communication to parents about the organization's scheduled activities.

Ongoing communication with parents is also important. Many organizations publish monthly or quarterly calendars of organizational events to keep parents informed of official activities. This list of events also helps establish the parameters of "official activities" for the organization, perhaps reducing the risk of, or providing the defense to, claims alleging organizational sponsorship of activities clearly beyond the nonprofit's control.

Be sensitive to the concerns of parents when problems arise.

At times, parents need to be consulted about their children because of accidents, injuries or problem behavior. The manner in which organizations approach parents in these situations can influence the probability of future legal action by the parents. Remember: People sue because they are angry, not simply because they are injured. Organizations would do well to keep this axiom in mind when conveying bad news to parents of children in their programs.

When informing parents of an injury, sexual molestation, or even, the death of a child, the organization's representatives need to empathize with, not be condescending to, the parents. Recognizing the emotional pain of the parents and offering genuine concern and support aren't only appropriate responses, but they are in the best interests of the organization. With properly trained staff members, this can be done without admitting legal culpability. Defensiveness and laying blame on the parents may serve to invite a lawsuit, which isn't the direction the organization wants to head.

Here are some proven strategies used by some organizations to involve parents in their programs:

- Assign volunteers to visit with the parents and explain the program and the organization's expectations.

- Create a fact sheet that explains the parameters of the program and what parents should do if the program violates any of the parameters. Have the parents sign the sheet acknowledging that they've read and understand.

- Send monthly schedules of events to inform parents what sponsored activities are planned.

- Include a parent's guide as part of the organization's published materials.

- Ask parents to talk with their children about child abuse and provide some structure for those discussions.

- Encourage parental participation, visitation and observation during the organization's activities.

The next chapter will address the maltreatment of children and what youth-serving organizations can do to protect their charges and themselves from harm.

Chapter 4
Child Maltreatment

A torn jacket is soon mended; but hard words bruise the heart of a child.
— Henry Wadsworth Longfellow

Trust, naiveté and inexperience are characteristics that recede as a child matures, but that make children vulnerable to victimization. Adults think to warn children against stranger-danger, but are less likely to admit the threat could be close to home or at home. Maltreatment may take the form of physical, emotional and sexual abuse or neglect.

Youth-serving organizations have two primary responsibilities with respect to child maltreatment. They should:

1. exercise reasonable care to ensure that maltreatment doesn't take place in the organization's programs; and,

2. respond appropriately anytime there are grounds to believe that a child is being subjected to maltreatment irrespective of the source or the venue of the maltreatment.

Reflecting our broad approach to abuse prevention, the material here extends to all forms of child maltreatment rather than to a narrow definition of "child abuse." Although we follow the common practice of using "child abuse" very broadly, "child maltreatment" is the more accurate term for the full range of harm to children by their caretakers and other individuals in positions of authority. In its strict legal sense, the term "child abuse" can be unduly limiting.

The legal definition of "child abuse" differs from state to state. Laws typically distinguish between maltreatment by a person who is responsible for a child's care and maltreatment by anyone else. When an individual who isn't responsible for a child's care causes an injury, that act may be considered an assault rather than child abuse.

Moreover, organizations may be held legally liable for child maltreatment that doesn't fit the legal definition of child abuse. For example, spanking a child could result in a lawsuit. The organization might be held liable even though a similar spanking by the child's parents wouldn't be grounds for legal action.

Child Abuse and Neglect State Definitions

Visit the National Clearinghouse on Child Abuse and Neglect Information Web site, www.calib.com/nccanch, for an online database of state statutes, including each state's definitions of child abuse and neglect.

An individual or organization also may be held responsible for responding to maltreatment other than abuse. Understanding the types of abuse and their corresponding indicators provides a basis for determining whether to file a report with child protective services.

Protecting Young Participants in Your Nonprofit

To ensure that maltreatment doesn't happen in the programs offered by your organization requires employing a combination of risk management strategies. Some strategies will be related to the specific activities offered by your organization and some should be standard practice in any organization offering services to children or youth.

Consider many forms of child maltreatment as risk management concerns for your organization. Often allegations of abuse arise from inappropriate disciplinary techniques, inadequate preparation for activities, motivational tirades gone amok, or boundary violations between staff members and young participants.

Be prepared to take action to prevent child abuse within your programs, and to protect the children in these programs who may be abused outside of these programs — most often in the home by family members. Any child may become a victim of child maltreatment. It occurs in all socioeconomic and cultural groups.

Child abuse by the sexual partner of the child's unmarried mother is increasing. Because previously abused children are at a higher risk of being abused, youth-serving organizations might incorporate staff screening and staff training to identify potential risk factors from this source.

For most youth-serving community organizations, the problem of child sexual abuse has become the lightning rod maltreatment issue. There are several reasons for this. Child sexual abuse is:

- *emotionally charged*, as are most topics dealing with children and sexuality,

- *extrafamilial* (in the context addressed by most community-serving organizations) and, therefore, less controversial to address than intrafamilial forms of child abuse,

- *more sinister*, as it deprives victims of childhood innocence and because of its secrecy, is less amenable to detection from external signs,

- *clearly a violation of societal taboos*, whereas those taboos aren't as well defined for hitting or otherwise inappropriately disciplining a child, and

- *causing the major portion of abuse-related lawsuits* that are difficult to defend and which have resulted in large awards of damages against some organizations.

Necessary Preconditions for Sexual Abuse

Research by David Finkelhor indicates that there are four preconditions necessary for sexual molestation to occur:

1. *There must be an offender with the motivation to sexually molest the child.* Adult-child sexual behavior is a strong taboo in our society, therefore, for child sexual abuse to occur, the molester must have extraordinary stimulus to initiate the sexual molestation of the child.

2. *The offender must overcome internal inhibitions against molesting.* Because of the societal taboos against sexual molestation of children, in order to engage in sexual victimization of children, the molester must justify in his own mind a rationale for his behavior that is sufficiently strong to outweigh the risks of detection.

3. *The offender must overcome the external barriers protecting the child from molestation.* Because of the many perils of childhood — including sexual molestation — we generally attempt to ensure that children are supervised and their activities monitored in order to enable intervention and protection from harm. Child molesters must circumvent these protective measures and isolate the child in order to effect the molestation.

4. *The offender must overcome resistance by the intended victim.* Child molesters must offer incentives to their intended victims or, in some cases, use force to engage children in sexual activities. They use many different kinds of ploys to trick children into sexual activities; often they offer financial or other material rewards. All too often, it only takes feigned affection and a violation of trust.

Understanding these four preconditions is important to the risk management of child sexual abuse within your organization. Effective youth protection policies are designed to make certain that none of the four preconditions is allowed to exist within an organization's program. To eliminate individuals who are motivated to sexually molest young people, nonprofits should have a rigorous screening process. They need to use a proactive screening and training program to communicate the seriousness with which the organization views the safety of its members thereby reinforcing the internal inhibitions of potential child molesters. They need to have strong guidelines that establish the external barriers that keep young people safe while participating in their programs.

The organization needs to have a desire to find abuse regardless of the potential consequences and discomfort the revelation may cause.

Finally, organizations should have a quality education program for participants to alert them about the risks of sexual molestation and thereby increase their ability to resist.

A recent report from the University of New Hampshire's Crimes Against Children Research Center documents a dramatic reduction in both reported and substantiated cases of child sexual abuse. Between 1992 and 1998, substantiated cases of child sexual abuse decreased by 31 percent and the number of reported cases of child sexual abuse declined 26 percent, report Lisa Jones and David Finkelhor in *The Decline in Sexual Abuse Cases*.

The report posits several explanations for this decline, including changes in how cases of child sexual abuse are reported, a possible child-abuse backlash causing possible reporters to avoid filing reports, and the possibility that there has been a genuine reduction in the incidence of child sexual abuse. It's far too early to declare victory on child sexual abuse and move on to other areas of concern.

Youth-serving organizations will have to continue to exercise vigilance in protecting their service recipients from this societal problem. One way a nonprofit can facilitate child abuse reporting is to assign someone in the organization as the point person where any and all questions about possible abuse are directed. This individual must become knowledgeable about child maltreatment and have direct access to the organization's chief executive officer. This individual would be responsible for ensuring that all allegations of child abuse are reported to the appropriate child protective services agency, as well as to the organization's legal counsel, insurers and key board members. As a part of the responsibilities for this position, the individual would be charged with terminating the alleged perpetrator's relationship with the organization until Child Protective Services can complete its investigation. This system could work across all types of organizations, large and small, paid and voluntary staff.

Although sexual abuse has become the abuse-related issue receiving the lion's share of attention, other forms of abuse and neglect also require attention by youth-serving organizations.

Risk Reduction Measures

Organizations striving to reduce the risk of child maltreatment in their programs should think in terms of the "Four Ps of Youth Protection." These are personnel, program, premises and participants.

Personnel

The basis for selecting paid and unpaid staff should be written position descriptions. They identify the usual functions of a position and help to establish the qualifications of staff needed to fill the positions. In addition, a position description is useful for identifying risk exposures related to each position so that appropriate risk management strategies can be applied.

Staff screening

The goal of staff screening is to find the best possible applicant for the position. Obviously, the best applicant for youth-serving programs will be someone who doesn't constitute an identifiable risk to the children. The National Collaboration for Youth suggests that *all* individuals who work with children undergo a basic screening process. Their publication, *Screening Volunteers to Prevent Child Sexual Abuse,* recommends a basic screening process that consists of written applications, face-to-face interviews and reference checks. If the position involves long-term, unsupervised contact with children, the Collaboration recommends performing additional screening such as criminal history record checks.

There are no screening techniques that can, with certainty, identify all individuals who are potential abusers. You can, however, use the screening process to look for possible warning signs and to let prospective applicants know the seriousness with which the organization views the safety of children in its programs. For example, during the interview, discuss child abuse and the organization's reporting policies with the applicant. By informing prospective staff members that any suspected abuse will be reported to authorities for investigation, you are discouraging applicants from acting on any motivation they may have to maltreat the children in your program.

Some organizations use a series of "red flags" or factors to alert interviewers to look deeper into the applicant's experience and background. As with all generalizations, many characteristics that are common to those who pose a threat to children are also common to individuals who are great with children. Other than a person with a documented history as a child victimizer, a person shouldn't be ruled out of consideration based on a single factor. A pattern of these factors, however, could be cause for concern. For more information on screening issues and a list of "red flags," refer to *Staff*

Screening Tool Kit: Building a Strong Foundation Through Careful Staffing, by John C. Patterson published by the Nonprofit Risk Management Center.

You'll need to go beyond the basic screening process for some positions. Many states require criminal history record checks of camp counselors or child-care workers. Some volunteer organizations require criminal history record checks for volunteers serving in positions that require a close relationship with individual children, such as mentoring. Before using criminal history records, identify specific offenses that would disqualify an individual from working with children. State statutes in many states dictate this list by specific offense code numbers. Many otherwise good volunteers, who may have criminal history records with convictions for minor offenses or for offenses unrelated to their qualifications for working with children, may be rejected if the screening criteria are overly broad.

According to the National Collaboration for Youth, many youth organizations agree that applicants who match any of the following criteria should be disqualified from staff positions working with children.

1. *Failure to complete the screening process.* Require all applicants for paid or unpaid positions to complete the specified screening process. Failure to complete the process may indicate that there are circumstances in the applicant's past that could raise questions about his or her suitability for working with children.

2. *Past history of sexual abuse of children.* Individuals who have sexually abused children in the past should never knowingly be appointed to staff positions working with children. While therapy is helpful for some offenders, there are no certain "cures," and the risk of another act of child molestation is always present throughout the individual's lifetime.

3. *Conviction for any crime in which children were involved.* Endangerment of a child through involvement in criminal activity shows blatant disregard for the child's well being. Due to decisions by prosecutors pursuant to plea negotiations and evidentiary concerns, many child sexual abuse cases are filed as child endangerment or similar charges. Either way, individuals involved with a child in a criminal act shouldn't be given access to children that could enable future criminal victimization.

4. *History of violence or any sexually exploitive behavior.* Child molestation is an act of violence. It's, under the best of circumstances, coercive and dismissive of the child's rights. Studies indicate a strong relationship between other acts of violence, such as domestic abuse and sexual assault, and child abuse, including child sexual abuse. Individuals with histories that include violence or sexually exploitive behavior shouldn't be allowed to work in any capacity with children.

5. *Termination from a paid or volunteer position caused by misconduct with a child.* Not all child sexual-abuse complaints lodged

against volunteers or employees are referred to official agencies for investigation. Some organizations just dismiss the individual from the organization. An applicant terminated from another position due to allegations of misconduct with a child constitutes an unacceptably high risk for repeat behavior and shouldn't be accepted.

It's advisable for organizations to obtain permission from applicants for any record checking. The application form should include a statement (similar to the sample provided below) authorizing the organization to verify information provided by the applicant and to access criminal history records and other office agency records.

Sample Consent Form

(We invite you to consider adapting the form to meet the needs of your nonprofit. Always obtain legal review before using anyone else's form in your nonprofit.)

I, _____ (applicant's name), hereby authorize _____(name of agency/organization) to obtain information pertaining to any charges and/or convictions I may have had for violation of municipal, county, state or federal laws. This information will include, but not be limited to, allegations regarding any convictions for crimes committed upon minors and will be gathered from any law enforcement agency of this state or any state or federal government, or from third-party providers of information originally obtained from law enforcement or court records.

I understand that I will be given an opportunity to challenge the accuracy of any information received that appears to implicate me in criminal activities. To facilitate this challenge, I will be told the nature of the information and the agency from which it was obtained. It will be my responsibility to contact that agency. I further understand that until the _____ (organization) receives notification from that agency clearing me, my application will be deferred.

As an applicant for an employee or volunteer staff position, I hereby attest to the truthfulness of the representations I have made. Except as I have disclosed, I have not been found guilty of, or entered a plea of nolo contendre or guilty to any offense similar to those listed on the application. Further, other than for the offenses I have disclosed, I have not had a finding of delinquency or entered a plea of nolo contendre or guilty to a petition of delinquency under the juvenile laws of this state or of any other state for any acts similar in nature to those listed on the application.

I further attest that I have not been judicially determined to have committed abuse or neglect of a child; nor do I have a confirmed report of child abuse or neglect or exploitation which has been uncontested or upheld administratively under the laws of this or any other state.

I understand that I must be truthful and, if any statement I have made is found to be false, I will be denied employment or volunteer placement or, if already accepted, terminated from my position.

_____ (Signature of the Applicant / Date)

Full Name of the Applicant: _____
D.O.B.: _____ Sex: ____ Race: _____ Sec. Sec. No.: _____
Driver's Lic. No: _____ State of Issuance: _____ Exp. Date: _____

A note of caution: Criminal background checks work as a deterrent for those offenders with records. More sophisticated offenders understand the system's weaknesses. The current system of background checks isn't comprehensive. Even with fingerprinting, the reporting by local authorities to a central directory is far from complete. In addition, the rate of conviction of acts of abuse against children is very, very low, thus making convictions a low source of protection against future abuse.

Staff training

Training is another important risk control measure for child maltreatment. Organizations have a responsibility to ensure that each staff member has the requisite knowledge and skills to perform the duties as specified in their position description. You also need to make certain that all staff know the organization's policies, procedures and guidelines, and how to implement them. To fulfill these responsibilities, organizations need to offer training to develop their paid and unpaid staff members' capabilities and knowledge.

Training may be held in classes or one-on-one with a coach or supervisor. The format isn't as important as the content. At a minimum, training for staff members working with children should include:

- how to recognize the signs of child abuse;

- how to recognize suspicious or inappropriate behavior;

- the policies the organization has relating to the care and supervision of the children in its programs;

- how to respond when there are reasonable grounds to believe or suspect that a child in the program is at risk of maltreatment; and

- the child development characteristics for children being served by the organization.

Training records should be maintained as part of each paid and unpaid staff member's personnel file. This is part of the record that demonstrates "due diligence" on the part of the organization and could be valuable when defending against claims alleging wrongdoing or negligence by the nonprofit.

Staff supervision

Staff supervision is another critical element for the prevention of child maltreatment in youth-serving organizations. Supervision can offer intervention to avoid child maltreatment and provide an objective witness if an allegation of abuse is lodged.

> The Nonprofit Risk Management Center publishes the *Staff Screening Tool Kit: Building a Strong Foundation Through Careful Staffing* (1998) that offers comprehensive information about screening processes. For more information, visit www.nonprofitrisk.org.

> *Due diligence* is taking any reasonable and necessary steps to ensure that the correct course of action is offered, or taken.

Staff supervisors for children's programs should be alert to signs of stress exhibited by individuals who work directly with children. Stress is a significant cause of inappropriate discipline leading to physical injuries of children. When supervisors detect signs of stress or stress-related behaviors, they need to intervene. It's far better to give a stressed-out staff member a few minutes to "get it together" and rest than to risk the staff member lashing out at a child who happens to be in the wrong place at the wrong time.

Staff supervisors also need to be alert to potential boundary violations by staff members. When observing the interactions between staff members and youth, supervisors should look for inappropriate physical contact, preferential treatment of some children, and violations of the organization's guidelines, i.e., avoiding one-to-one isolation of an adult with a child.

Suspension/Termination

When an allegation of child maltreatment is lodged against a staff member, the safest way to protect the children and the organization is to remove that individual from contact with any children in the program until the allegation has been investigated by an official agency. Because a suspension, termination or change of assignment can have legal repercussions, you should consult a lawyer to be certain that your actions are consistent with the laws in your jurisdiction.

Ideally, you will develop standard practices for dealing with allegations or suspicions of maltreatment in your organization before an incident occurs. Deciding what you will do before a crisis arises affords time to consider the consequences of each option. Moreover, following a standard procedure provides a defense against a claim that you treated an individual differently or unfairly.

Your policy may call for suspending the individual or assigning duties that don't include contacts with children until the charges can be resolved. Your policy on continuing to pay a suspended employee may depend on the law in your state and any applicable employment contracts or labor agreements. You generally have greater latitude in suspending or terminating volunteers, because employment laws don't ordinarily protect them.

Program

For the purpose of this discussion, *program* refers to the combination of activities, equipment and leadership that is integral to your offerings for young people. You may already address some of these items as matters of general health and safety.

Adult leadership

Proper adult leadership forms a strong barrier against child abuse; however, adult leaders are well-situated to be abusers. The suggestions offered in the "Personnel" section of this chapter form the first line of defense against abuse by adult leaders. Suggestions in this section provide additional protection.

Child maltreatment is less likely to occur when all interactions between adults and children are visible to others. Therefore, if private conversation is required, the youth and adult may move out of earshot of others, but not out of sight. This precaution helps to protect the adult from possible false allegations of abuse, while protecting the child from possible abuse.

Depending on the nature of the program, you might prohibit entirely one-to-one isolated contacts between adults and youths. In order to implement this policy, you may need to redesign some of your traditional programs. For example, the Boy Scouts changed the condition that each boy meets privately with an adult counselor to study merit badge requirements. To reduce the potential for abuse, two boys work together in a "buddy-system" with one adult to complete merit badge requirements.

In some organizations, a "two-deep" leadership requirement can reduce risks. "Two-deep" leadership calls for at least two adults to accompany children on overnight trips or campouts. This requirement works well for camping and sports programs with mainly group activities.

Mentoring programs, designed to promote one-to-one relationships between an adult role model and a child, require different strategies. Mentoring organizations can set up regular contact between supervisors and the children and their parents to determine whether children are satisfied and if they are having any problems with their mentors. In one case involving a mentoring program, a boy was abused over a six-year period. The boy's attorney alleged that for those six years no staff member asked the child about his relationship with his mentor. The only contact the program had with the participants was through the mentors themselves.

Visitors and staff family members

Employees and volunteers aren't the only potential abusers in a nonprofit setting. In a study of day-care centers, David Finkelhor and his associates found that staff members' family members committed a significant amount of the total abuse. While programs other than child-care centers haven't been as thoroughly studied, similar patterns are likely.

Several strategies can reduce this risk. The safest, but often impractical, policy is to prohibit contact between children in your programs and individuals who aren't subject to your screening, training and other abuse-prevention safeguards. Even if you instigate this policy it's moot if employees or volunteers take children home. Then other members of their households may need to be screened.

An intermediate approach is to provide family members and visitors with guidelines on acceptable conduct, and warn them that you will enforce the rules. Guidelines may limit contact with children and require that staff directly supervises any contact that does occur. Another policy might prohibit some or all visitors from helping children to change clothes or perform other sensitive tasks.

Parental involvement

Parents need to be involved in the activities of your organization and in your efforts to protect their children from harm. Use meetings with parents to inform them about the topic and steps they can take to protect their children from abuse. You can provide them with materials to share with their children to help them understand unacceptable behavior and how to report it. You can provide a contact person for parental questions and concerns and invite parents to connect with the organization. Good communication between parents, programs and youth is an effective abuse prevention strategy.

Allowing parents to visit their child's program at any time without an appointment significantly reduces the risk of abuse. In a study of abuse in child-care centers, David Finkelhor and his associates found much lower rates of abuse in programs that encouraged parents to drop in for unannounced visits.

Initiation rites for "secret societies," or special groups within groups, whose activities aren't supposed to become public can easily become a guise for sexual abuse. To reduce risk, these groups, if not prohibited, should be subject to parental observation.

Activities

Activities such as rock climbing, wilderness survival camps and athletics contribute to the development of self-confidence. If, however, the children participating in these activities are subjected to extreme pressure, ridicule, questions about their masculinity or femininity, or other forms of psychological degradation, the effect may be the opposite of the intent. The resulting destruction of self-confidence is emotional abuse. In addition, goading children to accomplish an activity beyond their abilities may lead to physical injuries. Participants should be adequately prepared both mentally and physically for the activity. Your failure to recognize the risks inherent in your program's activities can lead to injuries, emotional trauma and even death.

Whatever activities your organization sanctions, the guidelines for what is and isn't an approved part of the program should be clear. Child molesters may use organized youth programs to establish a legitimate contact with a child. The molester then initiates activities that are beyond the scope of the program with the child. For instance, a tutor may offer to extend the sessions after school hours and away from other adults. Parents and children should know whether that offer is proper or a ruse. By sharing programmatic guidelines with leaders, parents and program participants, you can not only thwart a molester, but where patterns develop, you can identify him or her.

Ideally, organizations should have adequate controls or not initiate a mentoring program. A molester will seek out programs that leave children vulnerable. Weak mentoring programs might be characterized as those with poor case management practices that fail to maintain regular contact with both the mentors and the mentees. There are many different styles of mentoring programs, and organizations initiating such programs should evaluate carefully their capacity to oversee the mentoring model that they select.

Volunteer enrollment and screening procedures in mentoring programs need to be designed to be effective to the level of trust and exposure presented by the program design. In other words, mentoring programs done on-site, where activity and contact are limited to a school, youth facility, corporate site or other fixed location, require less screening if on-site supervision is available. Community-based programs, where the activity is primarily outside of direct supervision, require adequate levels of staff training and program structure to fully trust the mentor to be responsible for the safety and well-being of the youth being mentored. The program structure can't depend solely on volunteer selection and screening but must include ongoing contact and support for the volunteer, child and parent by program staff or trained volunteers to assure the positive development of the mentoring relationship.

While it's true that the vast majority of adults don't present risk of abuse of children, be mindful that youth-serving programs are often targeted by individuals who are seeking access to children for illegitimate purposes. Programs need to be adequately designed and funded to be able to both select the adults that will develop a positive relationship with the children in their care and monitor these relationships. Since no screening or selection process is perfect, program design must include ongoing support and monitoring to identify any failures of the selection process and to identify lifestyle changes for the mentor that create new risks for the youth involved. For example, following her divorce, a mentor may move into the apartment of an abusive boyfriend whose history of violence was not considered when the mentor was initially screened by the nonprofit.

Photography

Photography is a favorite tool of child molesters. A molester may build a special relationship with children and gain their trust through photo sessions as a first step toward seduction. Or the photography itself may be abusive. In one case, a counselor at a church-operated camp coaxed several teen-aged boys into posing nude in scenes depicting various sexually explicit activities. The counselor used the camp's cameras and darkroom equipment. Authorities found several thousand slides of campers in poses that legally would be considered child pornography. This case presents an extreme situation. The following scenario in which a group of boys and their leader were on a backpacking trip in the wilderness is more typical.

> The day was hot and the boys decided to go "skinny-dipping" in the creek. The leader pulled out his camera and made some photographs while the boys were swimming. When he returned to the city, he sent the film out to a developer for processing. The film processor saw the nature of the photographs and reported the leader to the police. The police questioned the leader about the pictures and then questioned the boys from the trip.

> One of the boys voiced his embarrassment about the pictures and told the police that he didn't know the leader had taken them. The leader used poor judgment. Although the police determined that the photographs didn't fit the legal definition of child pornography, one boy's parents were outraged and filed a lawsuit against the leader and the organization.

If both organizations had guidelines governing photographing children, and educated staff, parents and participants about them, they might have prevented these situations. Informing parents and staff about the purpose of the policy may increase their acceptance of it.

Youth Leadership

Many youth programs are designed to provide opportunities for young people to develop leadership skills. In summer camps, these positions are commonly designated as counselor-in-training or CIT positions. They may be designated as youth aides in recreational or youth sports programs. In most cases, the youth in these positions assist with program leadership under the direct supervision of adult employees or volunteers. Sometimes these young people are so good at providing assistance that they are given inappropriate responsibilities that eclipse their training and maturity.

Organizations have a responsibility to protect all of the children they serve, including those who are in volunteer, youth-leadership development positions. The responsibilities of junior leaders should be designed to provide them with growth opportunities — developing leadership skills and learning job skills that can be applied in similar positions in other organizations The organization shouldn't exploit these youth, nor place them in situations that increase the risk of victimization.

When youth are assigned leadership responsibilities for other children, adult leaders should supervise their actions. Adults should monitor the leadership techniques used by junior leaders to ensure that they are positive and not punitive. If a child in the program must be disciplined, the adult should have the responsibility for administering appropriate disciplinary measures. Under no circumstances should a youth aide be permitted to spank, hit, slap or otherwise administer corporal punishment.

Youth placed in a junior leadership position may, by virtue of the position, exercise considerable influence over younger and less mature participants. This power differential may increase the possibility of sexual abuse by the youth leader. To prevent this, you need to ensure adequate supervision by adults and educate junior leaders to reinforce the boundaries of acceptable behavior. (Because most child molesters begin molesting as adolescents, consider identifying a counselor or mental health program where you can refer staff with abusive tendencies for help.)

Premises

The premises where a program takes place can invite abuse or limit abusers' opportunities to prey on children. Exits and entrances, lighting, and bathroom facilities are areas with inherent risk for the program and its participants. Several features of the premises, such as lighting and hot water temperature, can be controlled to reduce injuries that may be considered to be the result of abuse or neglect.

Access

Controlling access to areas where children are present protects them from harm by outsiders. If the program is housed in a building, a single point of entry is ideal, although not always feasible. At residential camps, schools, and other large facilities, visitors could be directed to a central point for signing the visitors' log and receiving a visitor's nametag. The safety of the children requires that individuals not be allowed to wander through the area without the staff's knowledge. Even smaller programs may benefit from signing visitors in and out and providing nametags and guides so that a visitor's status is clear.

Lighting

Adequate lighting deters wrongdoing. The lighting in hallways, walkways and parking lots should be bright enough to enable participants to identify individuals as they approach and to permit observers to recognize abnormal situations. When lighting is installed, it must be maintained in working order. Installation itself indicates the need for lighting. The failure to maintain these items could form the basis of a lawsuit alleging negligence. Assaults, car jackings, rapes and other offenses are more likely in the dark.

Shower and toilet facilities

Molesters frequently target children in shower-room and toilet factilities. A study of child sexual abuse in day-care programs, found that two-thirds of the cases occurred in a bathroom. Helping a child use toilet facilities gives an abuser an excuse to be alone with the child and dupe him or her into permitting genital contact. Bathroom design, especially for young children, can reduce the potential for abuse. David Finkelhor's study team recommended that toilet stalls for young children be designed to provide privacy for the child using the toilet, but permit observation by adult helpers.

Other forms of non-familial child abuse haven't been as well studied as child sexual abuse in day-care programs. In general, children are more vulnerable to sexual abuse in situations in which they are changing clothes, showering or otherwise unclothed. Being undressed will stop many children from running away to avoid the abuse. The risk escalates when a naked child is also isolated from other children or is alone with a single adult.

If the children in your programs represent a wide range of ages and developmental stages, think about scheduling showers and locker-room use at different times. This will minimize the opportunity for older, more mature youth to emotionally, physically or sexually molest younger children.

You should also consider separate shower facilities or separate shower times for staff. This division helps protect staff privacy and avoid situations in which allegations of sexual abuse could take on added credibility.

Participants

In addition to the strategies recommended above for addressing risks, policies centered on the children can reduce the risk of abuse. The policies discussed in this section establish operational boundaries regarding interactions with children. This resulting "personal protective shield" reinforces the measures suggested in the previous sections of this chapter.

Abuse-prevention education

Although children should never be solely responsible for their own protection from dangerous adults, they can protect themselves to some extent if they receive proper training. Children can be taught to recognize when someone is attempting to abuse them and to be alert to situations that leave them particularly vulnerable. They need to be empowered to resist abuse and to seek help from an adult to stop abuse. However, adults need to be trained to be sensitive that children don't always, even when trained, have the proper language to describe the abuse or ask for help. They may test the adult with an innocent question (What would happen if a friend …?) to gauge the adult's receptiveness before revealing abuse. Adults need to know to listen for the cues.

Out-of-program contact

Child molesters often use youth-serving programs to meet children. Once they have established contact through the program's legitimate activities, they expand their relationship with vulnerable children and eventually molest them. You can reduce this risk in your organization by adopting clear policies regarding out-of-program contacts between staff and participants. For example, you may wish to prohibit staff from baby-sitting for children participating in your programs. If it's impossible or impractical to prohibit staff from accepting out-of-program childcare positions with children in your program, the organization needs to clarify to the children's parents that the organization discourages such arrangements, and the parents need to exercise the same degree of care that they would for anyone employed in such positions.

The critical element in limiting out-of-program contact is delineating between what a sanctioned activity is and what is clearly not part of the organization's program and therefore, not the organization's responsibility to supervise. Once such policies are in place, communicate them to the staff, youngsters in the program and their parents. If they all know what's expected of them, they're more likely to comply. Violation of guidelines merits follow up to determine the level of concern and appropriate consequences to be taken.

Discipline

In most instances, the activities of youth programs are sufficiently rewarding that children want to behave. Sometimes, though, children misbehave, which can result in injury to themselves and others. To minimize the risk, every youth-serving program needs to exercise a reasonable degree of control over the participants. Appropriate discipline maintains order and protects children from injury.

Prohibiting physical punishment of participants by staff creates a buffer zone to protect children. Staff members and parents don't have the same options when disciplining children. Parents may choose to use physical punishment that doesn't physically injure their children. When a staff member hits, slaps or spanks a child, the action may be considered abusive.

Forbid your staff from withholding food and water as a disciplinary measure. Dehydration is a major health risk for children. Those participating in sports or other activities involving strenuous physical activity should have free access to water.

Program staff should be role models for exercising self-control. "Discipline" that results from staff anger or frustration may be abusive. Stressed-out staff may increase children's stress level, which in turn increases stress for staff.

Any disciplinary measure should be constructive. Discipline should always be an answer to a need of the child rather than a response to a need of the staff.

Touching

To touch or not to touch children while providing services to them is a topic of great consternation to the staff of youth-serving organizations. On one hand, they want to provide what children need — wholesome affection. On the other hand, touching can lead to claims alleging that the touching was improper. To make the issue more complicated, appropriate touching may lead to inappropriate touching as familiarity increases.

The following example illustrates how easily a touch can be misconstrued. As a group of children returning from camp in California were getting off their bus, one of the staff members noticed that a girl had a bit of mud on her skirt. Almost by reflex he reached up and brushed off the mud. When the girl arrived home, she told her mother that the man had touched her. Her mother reported the incident to the authorities. The man was arrested on suspicion of child sexual abuse, and the camp director who witnessed the act was arrested for failing to report abuse. Eventually all of the charges were dropped, but the memories of the bad experience live on. Scared by such incidents and the prospect of lawsuits, some organizations have instituted a "no touch" policy.

Some children literally demand physical affection. They may cling to their adult supervisors or teachers; some fight every attempt the adult makes to disengage from their grasp. Educate adults in your programs to use these opportunities to teach children that there are social boundaries to the expressions of physical affection. Adults in these situations can be role models to help children learn how to set boundaries for themselves.

Nonprofit Risk Management Center

47

Many youth-serving organizations offer programs in which physical contact between adults and children is almost unavoidable or absolutely necessary to fulfill the program's mission. Teaching children to swim or to use a balance beam may require some touching. Even in these programs, the risk of abuse or a false allegation of abuse can be minimized by reinforcing the child's right to set limits. If the activity is going to involve touching, let the child and parents know and instruct the coach or helper to tell the child in advance what is going to happen.

To see how this might play out, re-examine the case of the little girl with mud on her skirt. Rather than succumb to the reflex reaction to fix the situation, the adult could point out the mud and suggest that she brush it off. If she is unable to do this, the adult could ask her if she'd like him to brush it off. If she says, "No," then he should leave it alone. He would have honored her limits and given her an example to follow.

Some activities that require physical touching may need to be redesigned to eliminate an adult's touching that could quickly become inappropriate. Take the case of the high school wrestling coach who insisted on being the practice partner of the state-wrestling champion. When the student accused the coach of repeatedly groping him during practice, he was told that he must have been misinterpreting the coach's actions. Eventually the coach was fired, but the string of incidents need never have occurred. There were plenty of wrestling team members available to practice with each other. There was no legitimate reason for the coach to be a practice partner with one of the team members.

Touching Policy Guidelines

The following considerations can help you develop or review your own policy on touching:

- ❏ Touching should be in response to the need of the child and not the need of the adult.

- ❏ Touching should be with the child's permission — resistance from the child should be respected.

- ❏ Touching should avoid breasts, buttocks, and groin.

- ❏ Touching should be open and not secretive.

- ❏ Touching or other physical contact should be governed by the age and developmental stage of the child. (Sitting in an adult's lap may be appropriate for a three-year-old, but less so for an eight-year-old, unless the adult is the child's parent.)

Children need to have the right to say no to physical contact. A youth-serving organization can help the child understand and exercise that right. One approach developed by Cordelia Anderson, a veteran child-abuse prevention educator, was the concept of the "touch continuum." Anderson distinguishes between clearly good touches — those that are nurturing and proper and feel good; and clearly bad touches — those that feel "icky" and the child wants to have stopped. But there are also a large number of touches that are confusing — they may have felt good when they started, but at some point they began to make the child uncomfortable. A simple example is a warm hug that after the initial squeeze goes on and on and on.

Privacy

Children have a right to their privacy. Adults should respect children's privacy within the confines of health and safety requirements. The nature of the privacy right changes with the child's age and capacity to care for him or herself. Older children shouldn't be observed when changing clothes, showering or using toilet facilities unless security dictates that an adult be present. To set a good example and reduce opportunities for either abuse or misunderstandings, adults should also protect their own privacy in these situations.

Appropriate privacy policies differ depending on specific circumstances. Children with some kinds of disabilities may require extra adult assistance for taking care of their bodily functions. Even when extra care is needed, assistance can be provided with a mature, professional attitude by a trained staff member sensitive to children's need for privacy and for maintaining their dignity.

How to Say "No"

Children and adults in your organization have the right to say "No!" to unwanted expressions of physical expression. They also have the right to set boundaries for themselves. It's best if they can maintain the other person's dignity while rejecting his or her advances, but they must be comfortable with protecting their own boundaries nonetheless.

Some statements they can use are:

"Stop hugging (kissing, touching) me now."

"I don't like that."

"I'm uncomfortable when you ..."

"I would rather you..."

"Let's hug like this." (Then demonstrate the correct way to hug.)

"It's nice to be liked, but I'm uncomfortable when you cling to my leg. I'd prefer you just give me a quick hug to show that you like me."

Sign-in/sign-out procedures

Marvin Reinke, former president of YMCA Services Corp., states that some youth-serving programs are more careful about checking equipment in and out than they are about children's comings and goings. Carefully administered sign-in/sign-out procedures can protect against children leaving the site with an unauthorized person and provide an opportunity to verify that children arrive when expected.

Instituting a sign in/sign-out procedure requires each child's parent or guardian to identify the individuals authorized to pick-up their child from the program. Before a child is released from a program, the identity of the individual picking-up the child is checked against the list, and their identity verified, as needed.

A sign-in procedure also provides an opportunity for assessing the condition of children as they arrive. Conducting a visual inspection of the child — checking for bruises, cuts or other injuries — when greeting the child or helping with coats and mittens can be a part of the arrival activities for programs involving young children. Check-in is also a good time to note if the child appears to be healthy, is appropriately dressed for the season and meets reasonable standards of personal hygiene. This may seem overzealous; however, several organizations have been accused of maltreating children, when signs of abuse weren't detected until after the children were admitted to the program.

Recognizing Child Neglect and Abuse

One difficulty in recognizing neglect and abuse is that many of the signs are ambiguous. A child may have gotten a bruise from being beaten by an adult or by having run into a soccer goal. An adolescent may have contracted a sexually transmitted disease through sexual molestation or through consensual sexual activities with a boyfriend or girlfriend.

Another difficulty in determining maltreatment is that children respond to it in different ways. Some children show no behavioral signs of abuse, while others have dramatic changes in behavior.

One thing is certain, a sudden change in behavior, sustained over a period of time, suggests that the child needs assistance. The reason may or may not have to do with abuse or neglect.

Childhood stress may be triggered by many events — death of a family member or pet, divorce, school pressures, boyfriend or girlfriend problems, or abuse or neglect. Familiarity with the child helps in interpreting any of the signs you observe.

Educate your staff to identify indicators of childhood stress and what to do when they observe a child exhibiting signs of stress for more than a few days. They might appropriately ask the child if there is a problem. An open-ended question, such as, "Why have you been looking so sad lately?" or "You seem so angry; what is getting you all worked up?" It may also be appropriate to call the parents' attention to the behavior changes and talk to them about the staff's observations. Good ongoing communication with children in your program is one of the best prevention

Signs of Childhood Stress

❑ *Dramatic changes in school performance* — a sudden drop in participation or grades, a punctual child becoming tardy or skipping school.

❑ *Changes in behavior* — either regressive, in which the child reverts to behavior typical of a younger age, or precocious, in which the child acts much older than his or her chronological age.

❑ *Sleep disturbances* — nightmares, insomnia, fear of the dark, fear of sleeping alone or excessive sleeping.

❑ *Changes in eating behavior* — anorexia, bulimia, and sudden increases or decreases in appetite.

❑ *Inappropriate fears* — fear of a person, familiar place or activity.

❑ *Hostile language or aggressive behavior* — swearing, verbally wishing harm to others; or tripping, pushing, hitting, biting.

❑ *Overly compliant behavior* — willing to do whatever is asked, even if it's harmful to the child.

❑ *Depression* — hopelessness, withdrawal from family or friends, threats of or attempts at suicide.

❑ *Delinquency or running away from home* — stealing from friends, shoplifting, spray-painting graffiti on buildings.

activities. The interchange also increases the likelihood that if abuse does occur, early detection and intervention will be available.

In some situations the signs of abuse or neglect are very strong, or the child tells you or a staff member specifically about abuse. Then you must immediately take appropriate action, including filing a report of suspected abuse with the proper child protective services agency.

Neglect

Neglect occurs, says Douglas Besherov in *Recognizing Child Abuse: A Guide for the Concerned*, when a person responsible for the child's care withholds food, clothing, shelter, medical care or education. In order to be classified as neglect, the caregiver must have the financial means to provide these basic necessities. While most child neglect occurs in a family home, it can also occur in residential care settings, group homes, foster care programs, residential treatment facilities, summer camps and, especially, facilities serving children with disabilities.

When child neglect is severe enough to threaten the child's well-being, state law may require a report to child protective services. The following lists describe some of the behavioral, physical, and environmental indicators of child neglect.

Behavioral indicators of neglect

■ *Chronic hunger.* Child comes to school or other programs hungry and may not have a sack lunch even when explicit instructions were sent home to the caregiver. When a sack lunch is provided by the caregiver, it doesn't meet minimal nutrition standards.

■ *Pattern of truancy and tardiness for school, as well as other programs.* The adult caregiver fails to provide adequate control and discipline for the child.

■ *Child always appears fatigued or listless* due to inability to get adequate sleep, possibly caused by poor sleeping accommodations or failure of adult caregivers to enforce bedtimes.

■ *Dependence on others for meeting basic needs.* Child becomes a ward of the neighborhood, forming attachments with those who can provide food, clothing and shelter. This arrangement may result in a dependent relationship that increases the child's vulnerability to exploitation.

Physical indicators of neglect

■ *Poor hygiene.* Other children begin to avoid neglected children because "they smell bad."

- *Inappropriate clothing for the season.* Child may show up at activities without a jacket in the winter or dressed too warmly in the summer.

- *Unattended medical and dental problems.* Child may not see a physician or dentist when needed, or if medication has been prescribed, caregiver won't oversee its proper administration.

- *Developmental disorders.* Children don't develop normally, either physically or emotionally. Child may be smaller than normal and be verbally or emotionally unresponsive.

Environmental indicators of child neglect

- *Unsanitary conditions.* The home or residential facility may be filled with accumulations of trash. Pet droppings and urine may be evident.

- *Lack of adequate supervision.* Children left in the care of other children younger than 12 years old, according to *Recognition of Child Abuse for the Mandated Reporter* by J. A. Monteleone.

- *Inadequate housing.* Too many people living in one place or several children and adults sleeping in the same bed, which leads to lack of privacy and possible sexual abuse of children.

- *Drugs and alcohol abuse prevalent.* Children's needs are secondary to caregiver's needs to obtain drugs. Drugs and alcohol may not be kept away from children.

The effects of poverty are difficult to distinguish from the conditions of child neglect. Child neglect should be reported when the condition falls below minimum community standards for child care and the child's physical or emotionally well-being is harmed or threatened with harm, according to Besherov.

Abuse

Child abuse can be physical, emotional or sexual, or a combination of any two or all three. The signs manifest themselves in many ways. Being alert to the indicators and weighing these against the normal aberrations in child development and those of the individual child will serve you in protecting the child and organization from harm.

Physical abuse

Physical abuse includes scalding, beatings with an object, severe physical punishment and violent shaking, according to *Understanding Child Abuse and Neglect* by the National Research Council. Physical abuse also includes human bites, slapping, shaking, and burning with cigarettes or other objects, according to Monteleone.

Behavioral indicators of physical abuse

- Signs of childhood stress (See page 50.)

- Conflicting or changing stories about how the injury occurred

- Delayed or inappropriate treatment of the injury

Physical indicators of child abuse

A child who has been physically abused may exhibit suspicious injuries. The injuries attributable to normal childhood "wear and tear" are usually found on the leading edges of the body — shins, elbows and forehead. Injuries associated with physical child abuse may be located in soft tissues of the abdomen or on the back, or on backs of arms and legs — places not usually affected by normal childhood mishaps.

- *Burns* — Burns that may indicate a child has been abused include cigarette or cigar burns on the soles of the feet, palms of the hands, the back or genital areas. Other burns associated with abuse are friction or tether burns on the wrists, ankles or around the neck caused by ropes used to tie the child. Wet burns on the hands and feet that appear to be glove-like or sock-like are caused by forcing the child to bathe in water that is too hot. Dry burns leave distinctive marks in the shape of the instrument used to inflict them, commonly electric irons, radiator grates and kitchen range heating elements.

- *Bruises* — Bruises of a variety of colors (black, blue, yellow, and green) that point up different stages in healing and thus infliction at different times often indicate abuse. Varied colored bruises on the abdomen, back or face are especially suspicious. Bruises, similar to burns, may also reflect the shape of the weapon used to inflict them.

- *Lacerations and abrasions* — Children usually have scraped knees, shins, palms or elbows—injuries that are very predictable. Cuts and abrasions in soft tissue areas on the abdomen, back, backs of arms and legs, or on external genitalia are strong indicators of physical abuse. Human bite marks, especially when they are recurrent and appear to be adult-sized, strongly suggest abuse.

- *Fractures* — Unexplained fractures generally signal abuse. A child with multiple fractures occurring at different times is almost certain to be a victim of abuse. Other signs include swollen or tender limbs and spiral fractures caused by jerking of the arms.

Emotional abuse

Emotional abuse may be the most common form of abuse in youth-serving organizations. Although emotional abuse can seriously harm a child, it leaves no physical scars and very little other evidence. The abuse is most often verbal, making it very difficult to detect. Children themselves may simply quit a program, if they can, rather than either submit to the abuse or report it.

The five forms of emotional abuse listed by James Garbarino in *Emotional Maltreatment of Children* cover a wide range of actions. Each can hurt a child and some can lead to lawsuits.

- *Rejecting* — belittling, degrading and other forms of overtly hostile or rejecting treatment; shaming and or ridiculing the child for showing normal emotions such as affection, grief or sorrow; consistently singling out the child to criticize, punish or to perform most of the household chores; publicly humiliating.

- *Terrorizing* — placing the child in unpredictable or chaotic circumstances, such as witnessing domestic violence; placing a child in a dangerous situation; setting unrealistic expectations and threatening harm or danger if they aren't met; exploiting a child's fears and vulnerabilities; threatening violence against the child, the child's loved ones or objects.

- *Isolating* — confining the child or placing unreasonable restrictions on the child's freedom; placing unreasonable restrictions on the child's social interactions within the home or in the community or with another person responsible for the child's welfare.

- *Corrupting* — encouraging antisocial behavior such as criminal activities, prostitution, pornographic performances, or corrupting others.

- *Ignoring* — failure to express affection, caring and love for the child; being emotionally unavailable or uninvolved.

In most cases of emotional abuse, there are no physical signs of abuse.

Behavioral indicators of emotional abuse

- *Developmental disorders* — deficits in growth or development.

- *Habit disorders* — thumb sucking, head banging, rocking.

- *Conduct disorders* — antisocial or destructive behavior.

- *Reactive behaviors* — hysteria, phobias, compulsions and hypochondria.

- *Adaptive behavior* — inappropriately adult or infantile behavior.

- *Neurotic behaviors* — speech disorders and sleep disturbances.

- *Dramatic changes in school performance* — drop in grades, attendance problems or general functioning.

- *Suicidal behavior* — talking about suicide, threatening suicide or attempting suicide.

As with indicators for general childhood stress, these behaviors are indicators of a problem. The behavior may be caused by emotional abuse, or it may be induced by problems other than abuse. One way of checking is to call the parents' or caregivers' attention to the problem behavior and evaluate the reaction. If the parents reject efforts to help the child or their response is apathetic or indifferent, there may be grounds to make a report of suspected abuse, according to Besherov.

Sexual abuse

Sexual abuse occurs with children as early as infancy. This abuse isn't limited to penile penetration and encompasses acts that many of us have difficulty imagining. Nonetheless, molesters may commit any of the acts listed, which are based on the research of Kathleen C. Faller, a University of Michigan social work professor and a prosecution consultant on child molestation, who has been studying victims and perpetrators for 22 years.

Noncontact acts

- Sexual comments to the child on the telephone, in notes and letters, in person or through computer online services

- Exposure, such as the offender exposing his or her genitals to the child and masturbating in front of the child

- Voyeurism, in which the offender secretly observes the child for sexual gratification

- Showing pornographic material to the child

- Inducing the child to undress and masturbate in front of the offender

Note: Some readers may find the next few lists offensive — and they are. Imagine your discomfort at reading them and compare this to the discomfort of a child who experiences any of them.

Sexual contact (above or beneath clothing)

- Sexual contact includes: fondling or touching the child's genitals, breasts or buttocks; inducing the child to touch the offender's intimate parts; or rubbing his or her genitals against the child's clothing or skin (called frontage).

Penetration

- Penetration includes: digitally (finger) penetrating the child's vagina or anus; inducing the child to place his or her finger in the offender's vagina or anus; placing an object in the child's vagina or anus; or having the child place an object in the offender's vagina or anus.

Oral Sex

- Oral sex includes: tongue kissing; breast sucking, licking and/or biting; cunnilingus or the licking, kissing, sucking or biting of the vagina, or placing the tongue in the vaginal opening; fellatio or licking, kissing or sucking the penis; or anilingus or licking or kissing the anal opening.

Penile penetration

- Penile penetration includes: vaginal intercourse; anal intercourse; or intercourse with animals by offender in front of victim

Physical indicators of child sexual abuse

Physical evidence of sexual abuse, if present at all, tends to be temporary. These signs could include the following:

- Difficulty in walking
- Torn, stained or bloody underwear
- Pain or itching in the genital area
- Pregnancy
- Bruises or bleeding of the external genitals
- Sexually transmitted diseases

Behavioral signs of sexual abuse

The behavioral signs of sexual abuse are likely to be present longer and more conspicuously than physical signs. Many sexually abused children exhibit the signs of childhood stress (See page 50)) in addition to the behaviors associated with child sexual abuse.

- Exhibiting apprehension when sexual abuse is brought up
- Wearing lots of clothing, especially to bed
- Unwillingness to be left alone with a particular person
- Inappropriate understanding of sex for the child's age
- Fearing touch
- Drawing pictures with genitals
- Abusing animals
- Persisting in inappropriate sex play with peers or toys
- Cross-dressing

- Masturbating in public
- Engaging in prostitution

The presence of any of these indicators signals the *possibility* that sexual abuse has occurred. The indicators alone aren't conclusive evidence that the child has been molested.

Communication for Youth Workers

Sexual molestation and abuse is such a difficult topic for adults to deal with that they opt out. Many adults need encouragement to speak to their doctors or other adults about sexual difficulties or just plain sex; consider the plight of youth being victimized, many of whom feel they are to blame for the abuse. Youth workers need to be trained on how to communicate with youth on this topic and how to recognize and report signs of abuse.

Likely Victims and Offenders

Target Children

Some children are especially susceptible to becoming targets of abuse. Children with disabilities or other conditions that require caregivers to exert extra effort to meet their needs are especially vulnerable. Some caregivers reject these children, leading to neglect, emotional abuse and, in some cases, physical and sexual abuse. Other caregivers may resent having to make the extra effort and pass that resentment on to the child.

Children who are slow to become toilet-trained are more vulnerable to abuse. Some children are subjected to abusive ridicule or physical abuse, such as binding the penis to prevent urination or, after an untimely bowel movement, being severely burned by hot water when bathed by a caregiver.

Children who resemble a caregiver's spouse or other relative who excites strong negative feelings in the caretaker are more likely to be abused. Caregivers may transfer their hostility for the individuals with whom the child shares an unfortunate likeness to the child, according to Anne Cohn Donnelley in *An Approach to Preventing Child Abuse.*

When a Child Discloses Abuse

If a child becomes a victim of abuse, your initial reaction can be very important in helping him or her through the ordeal. The following guidelines may help you:

- ❑ *Don't* panic or over-react to the information disclosed by the child.

- ❑ *Don't* criticize the child or claim that the child misunderstood what happened.

- ❑ *Do* respect the child's privacy and take the child to a place where the two of you can talk without interruptions or distractions.

- ❑ *Do* reassure the child that he or she is not to blame for what happened. Tell the child that you appreciate being told about the incident and will help to make sure that it won't happen again.

- ❑ *Do* encourage the child to tell the proper authorities what happened, but don't promise to keep secrets because you may have to notify the proper authorities.

- ❑ *Do* consult a pediatrician or other child abuse authority about the need for medical care or counseling for your child.

Child Abusers and Child Molesters

Child abusers and molesters look like anyone else. They aren't identifiable by any readily observable physical, mental, psychological or behavioral characteristics — except that they mistreat children. Nonetheless, knowing the facts about abusers and molesters can help you design policies and procedures to prevent them from hurting the children in your nonprofit.

Individuals who mistreat children do so for a variety of reasons. One of the most common contributing factors is ignorance. Ignorance about any of the following areas increases the likelihood of neglect, emotional abuse and physical abuse by individuals who supervise children's activities:

- children's needs at various stages of their development,
- children's normal behavior or
- constructive disciplinary measures.

Stress also contributes heavily to abuse. Nearly 60 percent of child-abuse cases are related to stress, according to J.A. Monteleone. When the stress of looking after children is combined with social isolation, alcoholism and other forms of substance abuse, low self-esteem and unemployment, the risk of abuse rises sharply, according to the National Research Council. Beyond these factors, no distinguishing features identify most child abusers. Violent acts, including child abuse, are notoriously difficult to predict.

Child molesters, pedophiles & hebephiles

Child abusers who sexually molest children tend to be motivated by a desire for personal gratification. They are also much more likely than physical abusers to plan their exploitation of children. Several terms apply to individuals who are sexually attracted to children.

- Child molester — An individual who has sexually violated children.

- Pedophile — A clinical term for an individual with a compulsive sexual interest in children who haven't reached puberty. For this diagnosis, the sexual fantasy or feeling must have existed for at least six months and either have been acted upon or have caused severe distress to the individual, according to Judith Becker in her article, "Offenders: Characteristics and Treatment."

- Hebephile — An individual who has a compulsive sexual interest like a pedophile except that the preferred target is an adolescent.

Pedophile, in popular usage, often refers to any person who sexually molests a child or adolescent. This is technically inaccurate. Not all child molesters are pedophiles or hebephiles. There are other motivations for sexually assaulting children. Also, not all pedophiles and hebephiles are child molesters, since many haven't acted upon their fantasies.

Because most staff members of youth-serving organizations don't have the clinical credentials to diagnose pedophilia or hebephilia, the term *child molester* is preferred when discussing individuals who have sexually abused children — especially when presenting testimony in court. This term is based on observable behavior regardless of the cause of the behavior.

Stranger Danger and Other Myths

Resistance to accurately depicting individuals who are most likely to sexually molest a child impedes effective abuse prevention. Traditionally, child sexual abuse education programs have couched prevention messages in terms of "stranger danger." We seem to seek comfort in the idea that people who would commit such terrible acts are people we don't know.

These messages have contributed to the mistaken belief that strangers are most likely to sexually abuse children. In fact, strangers account for only a very small percentage of abusers. Characterizing child molesters as *strangers* is dangerous because children won't recognize the truth that any individual could be a child molester. It doesn't matter whether or not the child knows the person; what matters are the actions of the person toward the child.

Women Who Molest Children

Most child molesters are male, but about 30 percent of child sexual abuse occurs at the hands of women. According to David Finkelhor, a study of molestation in child-care centers found that women represented an even higher proportion of the abusers. Because abuse by women has been less common and less recognized, less is known about it.

However, more research results are focusing on women as perpetrators of sexual maltreatment. And more stories in the popular press are publicizing that women molest male children. Patricia Davin, Ph.D., a marriage and family therapist in Carson City, Nev., along with co-authors Teresa Dunbar and Julia Hisop, researched 76 women in prison for sex crimes. Their book, *Female Sexual Abusers: Three Views* reports that women are emotionally, not sexually, attracted to adolescent boys. The women they talked to are very vulnerable and desire to be wanted, loved and validated.

So even though there have been some breakthroughs in tracking the lives and motivations of female sexual abusers, the changes have only been in the past 10 years. The body of knowledge still focuses on the male offender. Consequently, most of the findings presented here pertain to men.

Myths About Child Molesters

Refuting myths about abuse and abusers provides a basis for developing suitable prevention strategies. These facts are based on the work of Nicholas A. Groth, Ann W. Burgess, H. Jean Birnbaum and Thomas S. Gary with sex offenders incarcerated in Massachusetts.

Myth: *Most child molesters are mentally retarded.*

Fact: Studies of people who molest children indicate that most (80 percent) have normal intelligence.

Myth: *Most child molesters are drug abusers or alcoholics.*

Fact: The tendency to molest children isn't caused by alcoholism or drug abuse. Some molesters do use drugs or alcohol to break down a child's resistance to involvement in sexual activities.

Myth: *Most child molesters are "dirty old men."*

Fact: Most child molesters commit their first assault during their teen years and continue until they are caught. It's true that most child molesters are men, but characterizing them as "old" is inaccurate.

Myth: *Most child molesters are insane.*

Fact: Most child molesters aren't psychotic nor do they meet the criteria for legal insanity. They know when they are molesting a child that what they are doing is wrong.

Myth: *Most child molesters are gay.*

Fact: Pedophiles who molest male children rarely identify themselves as gay and they are most often less likely to be aroused by an adult male than by an adult female.

Myth: *You can identify a child molester by the way he looks.*

Fact: Child molesters don't have any distinguishing characteristics that make them easily identifiable. Most appear as quite ordinary individuals who go to school, work and otherwise live in the community without calling attention to themselves.

Strategies Used by Child Molesters

Child molesters use three basic kinds of approaches to involve their victims in sexual activity: seduction, trickery and force.

■ **Seduction.** Child molesters may use forms of seduction that aren't appreciably different from courtship in adult relationships. The molester may begin by offering the child an unusual amount of attention. The initial overtures may be totally non-sexual in nature — perhaps an invitation to a movie or sporting event.

Child molesters who use seduction may become friends of the child's parents, and the parents may become unknowing accomplices in the sexual molestation of their children. Another common strategy is for the molester to befriend the staff, being the "special volunteer" who really cares. Over a period of time, the molester's attentions become more sexual in nature, until eventually sexual abuse occurs. Children may not realize that the activity is sexual abuse until after it occurs — sometimes years after it occurs. Child sexual abuse involving the use of seduction typically results in long-term relationships with repeated incidents of sexual abuse.

■ **Trickery.** Child molesters may use a ploy to trick the child into a situation conducive to sexual abuse. For example, a molester might offer a child a chance to be a movie star, but require that the boy or girl complete a screen test. Once the child is in the "studio" (perhaps a hotel room with an inexpensive video camcorder) and after pictures in clothes and swimming suits are taken, the child is told that the only thing between him or her and a Hollywood career is having some nude pictures taken.

Once the pictures are taken, they are used as leverage for further sexual abuse. Child molesters often use trickery to place the child in an isolated situation, such as asking a young child to help find a lost puppy near the playground. Trickery may be used in conjunction with seduction or with force. The molester may be known or unknown to the child. Trickery can result in a continued, sexually abusive relationship with the child or a one-time occurrence.

■ **Force.** The force used to molest a child may be either physical or psychological. Physical force is most common when the abuser doesn't know the child and commits the abuse on a single occasion (although there may be several occurrences over a short period). This is the stereotypical "stranger danger" scenario, and it's the least likely to occur. The danger of serious physical harm to the child is greatest in this situation.

Psychological force may be used with seduction or trickery, usually to ensure the silence of the victim and to maintain secrecy. Psychological force may involve threats against the child, the child's loved ones and even the child's pets. Psychological force may also be used to ensure continued access for additional sexual molestation of the child.

Children Who Molest Children

Approximately one-third of sexual molestation occurs at the hands of other children. Children may offend against their peers, younger children or even adults. Juvenile molesters are representative of all ethnic, racial and socioeconomic classes. Typically, children select a victim they know—most commonly a 7- or 8-year-old relative or acquaintance, according to Judith Becker.

Profiles of juveniles who are molesters document troubled lives with multiple problems, including delinquent behavior, poor social and academic functioning, and notably poor impulse control, says Becker. Unless they receive effective treatment, juvenile child molesters are likely to grow into adult child molesters.

Children in your care are vulnerable and require supervision by trained adults as they grow and mature. Knowledge of how children might be mistreated at various stages of their development and the strategies used by child molesters, as well as the characteristics of molesters, will help your staff be alert to ways to prevent harm from befalling them in your nonprofit.

The next chapter deals with violence among youth from bullies, gangs and weapons. It addresses how you can recognize threats and reduce their impact on your nonprofit's mission.

Chapter 5
Violence Among Youth

Violence cannot build a better society. Disruption and disorder nourish repression, not justice. They strike at the freedom of every citizen. The community cannot — it will not — tolerate coercion and mob rule.

— Commission on Civil Disorder, 1968

Violence pervades the lives of America's youth. The U.S. Centers for Disease Control reports that young people are the only segment of the population whose death rates have increased during the past 20 years, and most of those deaths are due to violent injuries and trauma. Nineteen percent of the deaths of school-age youth result from homicide, making it the third leading cause of death in this age group behind accidents and suicide. However, according to a study by the National Center on Institutions and Alternatives, the incidence of juvenile homicide is localized in that "six states account for more than half of the country's juvenile homicide arrests, and just four cities account for nearly a third of the juvenile homicide arrests. These cities, Los Angeles, New York, Chicago and Detroit contain 3.7 million juveniles, just 5.3 percent of the juveniles nationwide. Thus, cities that contain one in 20 juveniles nationwide account for one in three juvenile homicide arrests."

The U.S. Department of Justice reported in its October 2001 newsletter: Homicide is the only major cause of childhood deaths that has increased over the past three decades. In 1999, some 1,800 juveniles, or 3 per 100,000 of the U.S. juvenile population, were homicide victims — a rate substantially higher than those of other developed countries. At the same time, murders of juveniles are infrequent in many areas of our country. In 1997, 85 percent of U.S. counties had no homicides of juveniles.

In addition to fatalities, children experience considerable amounts of less serious trauma. David Finkelhor in his survey of 2,500 youths 10 to 16 years old found that 10 percent of the boys in the study had been kicked in the groin. Most of these incidents occurred in the seventh and eighth grades and 25 percent resulted in injuries. Boys with physical limitations, usually those who wore eyeglasses or had asthma, were three times more likely than other boys to be kicked. Forty percent of the assaults were by girls who said they were being harassed; the others were characterized as by bullies or by gangs in fights.

Surveys document that today's youth are aware of violence and feel less secure than those of the same age in previous generations. A 1997 study by M. Singer and his associates involving more than 3,700 adolescents in the 9th through 12th grades found that exposure to violence had a strong relationship with depression, anger, anxiety and disassociation. A 1999 study by the same researchers demonstrated the same strong relationship between violence exposure and post traumatic stress disorder (PTSD) symptoms in elementary school children (3rd to 8th grade).

The Centers for Disease Control reports that one of the first steps toward preventing violence is to identify and understand the factors that place young people at risk for violent victimization and perpetration. Previous research shows that there are a number of individual and social factors that increase the probability of violence during adolescence and young adulthood. Some of these factors include:

Individual

- history of early aggression
- beliefs supportive of violence
- social cognitive deficits

Family

- poor monitoring or supervision of children
- exposure to violence
- parental drug/alcohol abuse
- poor emotional attachment to parents or caregivers

Peer/School

- associate with peers engaged in high-risk or problem behavior
- low commitment to school
- academic failure

Neighborhood

- poverty and diminished economic opportunity

- high levels of transiency and family disruption

- exposure to violence

Organizations serving high-risk children must balance those children's need for services against legitimate concerns for the safety of all program participants.

A Three-pronged View

There are three aspects of violence that this section addresses: bullies, gangs and weapons. These three areas represent risk management concerns for youth-serving organizations. Understanding the nature and extent of the impact that these three areas can have on youth-serving organizations will enable them to implement more effective risk management strategies.

Bullies

Nearly all children come into contact with bullies. According to St. Petersburg, Fla., researcher and pediatrician Bruce A. Epstein in a story filed by MSNBC News, about 10 percent of children experience bullying on a regular basis. He states that "an estimated 4.8 million children are involved in episodes of bullying—2.7 million as victims and 2.1 million as bullies." If the behavior is allowed to go uncorrected, it can have serious consequences for the bully, as well as the victim.

Bullying goes beyond the single episode of teasing or fighting in which many children participate. It is, instead, a pattern of behavior in which the bully attempts to intimidate his or her victim. Examples of bullying behavior range from teasing or extortion to physical assault. The National Crime Prevention Council lists as characteristics that all bullies have in common:

- being concerned with their personal pleasure.

- wanting power over others.

- being willing to use and abuse other people to get what they want.

- feeling pain inside, perhaps because of perceived personal shortcomings.

- finding it difficult to see things from someone else's perspective.

Epstein reports that bullies generally are victims in their homes. Their parents tend to be aggressive and act out their frustrations with violent outbursts. Discipline is inconsistent, and usually physical, leading the child to believe that "might makes right." Often a bully's parents lack interest in the child, thus the child never learns appropriate behavior. Youth development organizations can be a positive influence for changing a bully's behavior. The attention lacking at home might be found at your organization once trust is established. Other programs also might be able to model or suggest other ways that the bully might interact with peers.

Left to their own devices, bullies may drop out of school and in extreme cases may be convicted of three or more criminal acts by the time they reach their 21st birthdays. As adults, bullies are more likely to work at low-skill, low-pay jobs, and they may become uncaring, punitive parents, thereby begetting a new generation of bullies.

Victims of bullies also have commonalties. The National Crime Prevention Council points out that anyone can be the target of a bully, but most often the victim is shy, sensitive, and perhaps anxious and insecure. Some bullies will target children for physical reasons, such as being overweight, physically small, having a disability or belonging to a different race or religion.

Openly gay and lesbian youth are often targets for bullies. An article in *Time*, Dec. 8, 1997, cites a Massachusetts study funded by the Centers for Disease Control that found that 62 percent of students identifying themselves as gay, lesbian or bisexual had been in a fight during the previous year as compared with 37 percent of all students.

Traditionally, we have characterized learning to cope with bullies as a part of growing up. Recent research indicates that being victimized by bullies may have lasting consequences. One way that children seek to stop victimization is to avoid the bully. This means not going to school, if that is where the victimization takes place, or not participating in activities where the bully is likely to appear. Some victims of bullying attempt to protect themselves by obtaining weapons — most commonly knives and firearms. In their desperation, a preemptive strike seems not only a reasonable step, but a necessary one, as well.

For example, James Garbarino relates the true story of a 15-year-old boy who was convicted of the murder of a bully. The bully had taken a gold chain from the young man. Two weeks after the bully had taken the young man's gold chain, he saw the bully wearing it. The young man approached the bully with a gun in hand demanding he return the chain. Even after the bully returned the chain, the 15-year-old boy put the gun to the 19-year-old's head and pulled the trigger. The younger boy felt that if he didn't kill the older youth, he would continue to be at risk. This victim's case is far from unique.

Victims of bullies often don't tell parents or other adults that they are being bullied. Therefore, adults need to be on the lookout for telltale signs.

Some of these are emotional withdrawal, a drop in grades, torn clothes, unexplained bruises, refusing to go to school, needing extra money or supplies, regularly "losing" toys or other possessions taken to school.

Gangs

The stereotypical media image for youth gangs is only partially accurate. According to the Justice Department, a gang is "a well defined group of youths between 10 and 22 years old." To be considered a "youth gang" a group must be involved in a pattern of criminal acts. The criminal acts, especially acts of violence, serve to cement the group together. Researchers Norman Randolph, Alan McEvoy and Edsel Erickson observe that "sharing the anticipation, danger, harm and excitement of a gang's exercise of brutality against outsiders creates feelings of a common identity and shared purpose." They go on to say, "Clearly, occasional acts of group violence define group boundaries, create or reinforce group identities, and bind members together in a common cause. Yet it's the shared vicarious reconstruction or anticipation of violence that is so much more relevant to bonding than is violence per se."

Howell points out that violent behavior "is not the only behavior in which gang members partake. For the most part, gang members 'hang out' and are involved in other normal adolescent social activities, but drinking, drug use and drug trafficking are also common."

Demographic studies of gangs cited by Howell show that the typical age range for a gang is 12 to 24 years old with 17 to 18 being the average age of gang members. The average age tends to be older in cities like Los Angeles and Chicago where gangs are well established and have been in existence for longer periods of time. Male gang members outnumber female gang members by a wide margin. Traditional gangs average about 180 members, while specialty gangs — drug traffickers — are much smaller averaging about 25 members. The ethnicity of gang members is 48 percent African-American, 43 percent Hispanic, 5 percent white and 4 percent Asian. The preponderance of African-American and Hispanic representation in gang membership isn't due to a predisposition of those ethnicities to gang activities, but rather an over-representation of those ethnic groups in areas most conducive to gang activities.

Many researchers give several motivations for joining a youth gang. These reasons include:

- enhanced status or prestige among friends.
- increased income from drug sales and other criminal enterprises.
- protection from other gangs.

■ social relationships giving a sense of personal identity.

■ coercion into joining.

Youth-serving organizations should be alert to signs found by researchers that indicate gang activity. One such sign is a "red flag"; two or more indicate careful scrutiny is needed. According to Ronald D. Stephens, executive director of the National School Safety Center at Pepperdine University in Westlake Village, signs of gang activity include:

❑ *Graffiti* — Gangs use graffiti to mark their territory. When another gang disputes territory they often cross out the rival gang's graffiti and replace it with their own.

❑ *Colors, jewelry and distinctive clothing* — Gangs generally establish distinctive clothing to signify affiliation with a particular gang. Unwary youths wearing similar clothing may become a victim of gang rivalries.

❑ *Physical confrontations and staredowns* — Increasing violence may signal the presence of gangs.

❑ *Beepers, pagers, and cellular telephones* — Youths who carry electronic communications tools may be involved with gang drug activity. But given the prevalence of beepers and wireless phones today, this sign alone is unlikely to indicate gang activity.

❑ *Drive-by shootings in the community* — Drive-by shootings are most often the result of competition between gangs for territory.

❑ *"Show-by" display of weapons* — Usually a precursor to drive-by shootings. Gang members will drive by brandishing weapons to demonstrate their capacity for deadly violence.

❑ *Racial conflict* — There is a high correlation between racial conflict and gang membership. Many gangs are formed along racial and ethnic lines for protection and affiliation.

❑ *Community history of gangs* — Communities with a history of gangs are more likely to have an established gang presence with gang membership including representation from several generations.

❑ *Increasing presence of informal groups calling themselves a "posse," "crew," or some other socially questionable name* — Informal groups with seemingly benign, yet revealing, names may be the first step to becoming involved with a gang.

❑ *Tattoos* — Gang members may have tattoos that symbolize their gang affiliation.

Weapons

Weapons are a cause of, as well as a response to, the violence that young people perceive in the world around them. In 1997, as part of the Youth Risk Behavior Surveillance System, the Centers for Disease Control and Prevention conducted a national school-based Youth Risk Behavior Survey that resulted in 16,262 questionnaires completed by students in 151 schools. The survey showed that nearly 20 percent of high school students reported carrying a weapon (gun, knife or club) in the prior month. Males are more likely than females to carry weapons and Latinos and African-Americans are more likely to than white students are, according to a Cox News Service article in the Aug. 14, 1998, *San Francisco Chronicle*. Often, young people carry weapons to protect themselves from the violence that they fear. There is a high correlation between carrying weapons and youth gang activity.

Many school systems and other youth-serving organizations have adopted a zero tolerance policy toward weapons—especially guns. The prohibition against guns in school settings is a requirement of the federal Gun Free Schools Act (GFSA) (PL 103 382) passed in 1994 that requires any student who carries a firearm to school to be expelled for not less than one year. The GFSA includes in its ban other explosive devices, including tear gas, pipe bombs and even starter pistols, which fire blanks. The requirements of the GFSA extend to any school that receives funds from the Elementary and Secondary Education Act.

Weapons' bans extend beyond firearms and explosive devices and include knives, slingshots, brass knuckles, blackjacks and hand-held personal defense sprays. Some weapons' bans have also applied to implements, such as nail clippers and combs with long pointed handles.

To detect weapons, schools and other youth-serving organizations use a combination of metal detectors and personal searches. Dress codes often ban the wearing of loose clothing, which can hide weapons. Some organizations and schools also ban large purses and backpacks or require that they be transparent.

Success-Oriented Conduct Codes

Young children, who think in concrete terms, need short, specific rules that they can understand, follow and know when they broke. A sample follows.

Rules of Conduct
❖ No hitting.
❖ No biting.
❖ No pinching.
❖ No slapping
❖ No kicking.
❖ No pulling hair.
❖ No fighting.
❖ No yelling.
❖ Report all accidents to your teacher (leader).

School-age children who comprehend abstract concepts, need direction, but can understand broader terms. A sample follows.

Rules of Conduct
❖ No fighting.
❖ No weapons.
❖ No drugs, including alcohol, or drug paraphernalia.
❖ No swearing or bad mouthing.
❖ Report all accidents to a teacher/leader.

The rules should reflect the developmental age of the program's participants.

There is a fine line between the implementation of policies to keep weapons out of your organization's activities and respecting the privacy and civil rights of the children in your program.

Risk Management Strategies to Reduce Violence

Just as with child maltreatment, the risk management measures necessary to control violence in your organizations' programs begin with the staff. Discipline is the first step the staff should take. If discipline doesn't get the young person to change his or her behavior, the next step is for the staff to speak with the parents. If the young person's behavior is still not acceptable, the staff should tell the parents that they will have to find services for their child elsewhere.

Discipline

The best control techniques reinforce positive behavior and don't reward bad, or negative, behavior. Smiles, an encouraging pat on the head, a word of encouragement, and other kinds of praise and support will often be all that's required to have the children or youths with whom you work ready to jump through hoops to please you. Unfortunately, the children that are most needy for words of encouragement or praise are the most problematic from a disciplinary perspective. These children are so much in need of attention that they are willing to misbehave to obtain negative attention rather than share attention with the group.

The disruptive behavior of individual children shouldn't be allowed to interfere with the ability of other children to benefit from your organization's services. Disruptive behavior may also put the safety of the child and possibly the safety of the entire group at risk. Discipline should address behavioral problems that impair the organization's ability to accomplish its mission.

When discipline of a child in your organization's program is necessary, the discipline should be age-appropriate and related to the behavior that you are trying to change. Slapping, hitting and spanking children are inappropriate disciplinary techniques for nonfamily caregivers. While of questionable value in a family situation, when these disciplinary techniques are used outside of the family, the risks of allegations of child abuse and subsequent lawsuits are considerable.

For younger children, a time-out corner with a chair for the child to sit for brief periods of time is appropriate. Two or three minutes in the time-out corner are usually all that is necessary for the child to contemplate his or her wrongdoing and be ready to rejoin the activity. A good rule of thumb is one minute for each year of the child's age. Longer periods of time in the time-out corner are counter-productive. If disruptive behavior continues, temporary exclusion from the group may be appropriate.

Running extra laps, doing pushups, and other physical exercises are common disciplinary measures in youth sports programs. Within reason, these may be appropriate as they allow the youth to expend some excess

---

SAMPLE

This form may be adapted to use with preteen or teenage participants in your program. You may wish to make the language less formal or the vocabulary less sophisticated, depending on the developmental stage of the young people in your programs. You might also wish to add or subtract components to the code. You may find you get more "buy in" if the participants are part of the development process. If you use a "contract" such as this, you must be willing to enforce the consequences if the code is broken, or otherwise the "contract" has no meaning for the participants. Including youth and staff together in one code strengthens the notion that rules are part of life that both youth and adults have to follow.

Participant Code of Conduct

[Name of Nonprofit] is a youth-serving, community-based organization dedicated to providing [description of mission or services]. Participation in the organization's programs is subject to the observance of the organization's rules and procedures. *The activities outlined below are strictly prohibited.* Any participant or staff member who violates this Code is subject to discipline, up to and including removal from the program.

- Abusive language towards a staff member, volunteer or another participant;

- Possession or use of alcoholic beverages or illegal drugs on [Name of Nonprofit]'s property or reporting to the program while under the influence of drugs or alcohol;

- Bringing onto [Name of Nonprofit]'s property dangerous or unauthorized materials such as explosives, firearms, weapons or other similar items;

- Discourtesy or rudeness to a fellow participant, staff member or volunteer;

- Verbal, physical or visual harassment of another participant, staff member or volunteer;

- Actual or threatened violence toward any individual or group;

- Conduct endangering the life, safety, health or well-being of others;

- Failure to follow any agency policy or procedure;

- Bullying or taking unfair advantage of any participant;

- Failing to cooperate with an adult supervisor/leader/mentor.

I have read and I understand the [Name of Nonprofit]'s Code of Conduct. I agree to abide by the rules described above and understand that I may be removed as a participant if I violate any of these rules.

Signature _____ Date _____

Witness _____ Date _____

---

energy and are consistent with the aims of the sports programs to promote fitness and physical conditioning. Their use, however, should be avoided when they could aggravate an injury or when climatic conditions could cause hyper- or hypothermia. Withholding water is never an appropriate disciplinary strategy.

Parent Conferences

Usually, only a few children are responsible for most of the disruptive behavior in an organizational setting. If your program has a chronic troublemaker, it may be necessary to have a conference with that child's parents. When conferring with parents, identify the objectionable behavior and the reasons the organization finds the behavior objectionable. Discuss the steps you have taken to control the child's behavior and the results. Refrain from making accusations and control your anger. Indicate that the behaviors are unacceptable and seek the parents' assistance. Some parents may try to shift the responsibility back to the organization by giving their permission to use corporal punishment or other more severe forms of punishment. This should be unacceptable. Let the parents know that if the disruptions continue, the child will need to seek services elsewhere.

Bullies, gangs and weapons represent risk management concerns for youth-serving organizations. The staff needs to be educated and alert for the first signs of disruptive behavior among program participants and take corrective action. It's important that requests for changed behavior are monitored and, if the young person fails to comply, that stated consequences occur.

Although violence commands the majority of child-injury media headlines, accidents cause the majority of child injuries. The next chapter will focus on injuries by source, such as poisons and falls, and injuries by site, such as playgrounds and camps, and some measures you can take to lessen the number and severity of these injuries at your nonprofit.

Chapter 6
Injuries and Accidents

Youth doesn't reason, it acts.
— Francis Picabia

Each year while sleeping, playing, eating, and exploring more than 14 million children incur injuries requiring medical attention. According to the National Injury Center for Prevention and Control of the National Centers for Disease Control, "20 to 25 percent of all children sustain an injury sufficiently severe to require medical attention, missed school and/or bed rest."

Children are at risk from falls, motor vehicle injuries (as occupants, pedestrians and bicyclists); drowning; fires and burns; choking, suffocation and strangulation; and poisoning. Most childhood injuries happen at the child's home or while participating in family activities — a fact that should give some small peace of mind to organizations that serve children and youth. How this will change as more and more children spend more time being cared for away from home, we don't know. If youth-serving organizations apply proper risk management strategies, it may not.

Although broken bones, sprained ankles, concussions, animal bites, knocked-out teeth, sunstroke and dehydration are unfortunately associated with activities for children and youth, as much as 90 percent of these unintentional injuries can be prevented through education, equipment modification, safe practices and supervision.

Your goal is to 1) prevent injuries from occurring and 2) diminish the damage caused if they do occur, and 3) limit the long-term effects of injuries. For example, prevent unintentional poisoning by storing poisonous material away from children's reach, educating older children not to eat or drink unknown substances, and keeping the poison control center's phone number readily available by all phones.

Examples of Injury Reduction Methods

- ❏ Energy-absorbing surface beneath playground equipment can prevent serious injury from falls.

- ❏ Seat belts can protect children from death in a motor vehicle crash.

- ❏ Polystyrene-lined helmets can prevent brain damage in bicycle accidents.

Many youth-serving organizations operate under the misconception that injuries only happen in sports programs. This just isn't true. All children in any setting are at risk of unintentional injury. Severity of injury varies with each child's age, development, environment and exposure to risk. Those at greatest risk are children who are 4 years old and younger, or male, or live in poverty or rural communities.

There are two ways of isolating the risk. One is to look at the source of injury: poison, burns, falls or bicycle riding. A second way is to look at the site where accidents occur: playgrounds, sports and recreational facilities, day care centers and summer camps. We have chosen to do both because each gives a different perspective of how to identify risks for your youth-serving organization.

Common Reported Injuries in Child-care Programs

- bites by other children
- choking on food
- fingers pinched in doors
- forehead cuts from falls
- insect stings
- minor and superficial head trauma
- minor dental trauma from falls and collisions
- minor fractures
- minor trauma to the mouth and lips
- nose bleeds
- other minor cuts
- scrapes and bruises from falls
- scratches from falling outside
- superficial injury from children colliding with each other

Source – *Injury Prevention and Control for Children and Youth,* American Academy of Pediatrics

Highest Injury Risks in Adolescence

Early Adolescence 11-14
- motor vehicle (unbelted passenger)
- unintentional injury from firearm use
- water sports injuries
- sports injury from bicycles, skateboards, running sports and baseball

Middle Adolescence, 15-17
- motor vehicle (driving late at night and weekends)
- homicide (impulsive)
- suicide (impulsive)
- drowning
- sports injuries from contact sports, football, basketball

Late Adolescence 18-21

❏ motor vehicle injury (driving drunk)

❏ homicide (cultural risks)

❏ suicide (from depression)

❏ work injuries (power equipment)

Source – *Injury Prevention and Control for Children and Youth*, American Academy of Pediatrics

Injury by Source

Falls

Falls remain the leading cause of unintentional injury for children 14 and under. From infants learning to walk who crash into furniture and tumble onto floors to older teens attempting to snowboard off a cliff who careen into boulders and trees, falls are part of testing the territory.

Falls accounted for 85 percent of playground injuries in a study reported by the Harborview Injury Prevention Research Center. One-third of these injuries related to the use of trampolines. The problem of trampoline use is of such significance that the American Academy of Pediatrics recommends that "trampolines should never be used in the home environment, in routine physical education classes or in outdoor playgrounds."

The Consumer Product Safety Commission (CPSC) found that slides were a frequent cause of falls for younger children and climbing equipment the most frequent source of falls for children older than six. The severity of the injury depends on the height of the fall and the surface on which the child lands. Standards exist for the height of slides, swings and climbing apparatus depending on the age and, thus, developmental stage of children. The CPSC publishes standards for the types of acceptable cushioning material, its depth (at least 12 inches) and its radius (at least six feet) under playground equipment.

All of the hazards for children aren't on the playground. The CPSC has documented head injuries and deaths of children due to television sets falling on them while moving a TV cart or, in one case, while climbing on a loaded TV cart.

Cuts are the most commonly treated injuries resulting from falls; fractures are the most common injuries in falls from heights. Fractures or dislocations and head injuries account for most of the hospitalizations from falls. Severe injuries and death from falls are usually related to head trauma.

In childhood, the highest risk of suffering a serious injury from a fall is during the first year of life; risk deteriorates with age. Boys fall more than girls; this difference in gender is noticeable after 4 years.

Motor Vehicles

Organizations have risk exposures when participants in their programs are transported:

- in vehicles owned by the organization,

- in vehicles, whether owned by the organization or not, but driven by staff or volunteers of the organization,

- by commercial vendors under contract to the organization.

While some vehicle crashes are caused by equipment malfunctions, by far the majority is caused by driver error. Distractions such as cell phones, radios, CD players and noisy or squabbling passengers exacerbate these problems. Another condition that places people at risk are drivers who are unfamiliar with the type or size of vehicle they are driving. Many organizations own their own school buses or large vans and use volunteers to drive. If the drivers don't routinely operate large motor vehicles, they may be unable to respond correctly to unexpected road hazards or mechanical failures. Some child-care organizations report fewer collisions subsequent to switching from 16-passenger to 12-passenger vans and credit the reduction to drivers being more familiar with a smaller size of vehicle.

The federal government, recognizing the risk to the public when unskilled or reckless drivers operate large motor vehicles, enacted a law requiring anyone operating a 16-passenger or larger vehicle to obtain a commercial driver's license, referred to as a CDL. The process used to obtain a CDL includes an extensive record check of past driving experience and drug and alcohol screening. These requirements apply to volunteer drivers, as well as paid drivers. Some states have even more stringent requirements. For example, in California, drivers of vehicles that carry 10 or more passengers including the driver, are required to have a DCL, also known as a Class B license. Check the law in your state to determine its specific requirements.

Some accidents are simply caused by carelessness. Accidents caused while backing up a vehicle are a case in point. This kind of accident can be avoided by using a spotter who assists the driver by looking at areas the driver can't see while backing up. Some organizations have found that the installation of vehicle alarms (such as those you hear on construction vehicles) that sound when the vehicle is backing up is a cost-effective way to avoid these accidents.

Unsafe vehicle condition also contributes to numerous collisions each year. Whether vehicles are owned by the organization, staff members, volunteers or third-party vendors, if used to transport participants in a nonprofit's programs, the organization should make sure that they are in safe operating condition.

No discussion of motor vehicles would be complete without touching on the problems of young drivers. Motor vehicles are one of the leading causes of injury and death of children and youth. The results of the *1997 Youth Risk Behavior Surveillance* conducted by the Centers for Disease Control show that many high school-aged youth engage in behaviors that increase their likelihood of death from motor vehicle crashes. These behaviors include:

■ not wearing seatbelts (about 20 percent said they rarely or never use seatbelts);

■ riding with a driver who had been drinking alcohol (more than one-third — 36.6 percent — had ridden one or more times with a driver who had been drinking);

■ driving after drinking alcohol (16.9 percent of students said that within the 30 days preceding the study they had driven a motor vehicle one or more times after consuming alcohol); and,

■ riding motorcycles without a helmet (36.2 percent of those who rode motorcycles said they rarely or never wore a motorcycle helmet).

Drivers 16 to 20 years old are at highest risk of dying in a crash, and males are twice as likely to die as females according to the American Academy of Pediatrics. High risk-taking behavior, a feeling of invincibility that is exacerbated by alcohol, illegal drugs and low-rate of seat-belt use contributes to injury and death in this age group.

All of these behaviors can affect organizations offering services to teens or who employ minors. The teens in these programs may bring a lot of pressure on the organization to permit them to operate a motor vehicle in conjunction with the organization's programs. Don't do it. "Teens are more likely than older drivers to speed, run red lights, make illegal turns, ride with an intoxicated driver and drive after using alcohol and drugs," according to the "Motor Vehicle-related Crashes Among Teenagers," fact sheets of the National Center for Injury and Prevention. They are also "more likely to underestimate the dangers in hazardous situations and have less experience in coping with those situations." As drivers, they may present a risk to themselves, their passengers, drivers and passengers in other vehicles, bicyclists and pedestrians.

Risk Management Strategies

When children are transported in vehicles owned or operated through your nonprofit, consider a variety of risk management strategies to reduce injury. The National Highway Traffic Safety Commission reported in 1996 that if the driver didn't buckle up, it was likely the child passenger wasn't buckled up. Thus, it's important to educate staff and volunteers who drive for your organization to "buckle-up" their young passengers and themselves before starting the vehicle.

In addition to wearing your seat belt, other safety precautions that used to be considered common sense for a driver and unnecessary to state, include:

- ❏ *radio volume* — Set the volume low enough so you can hear other people in the car shout a warning and the sirens of emergency vehicles.

- ❏ *wireless phones* — Whenever possible, pull over to use the phone. If you must talk and drive, use a hands-free set. When approaching heavy traffic, tell your party you must hang up until the situation is cleared.

- ❏ *horseplay* — Driving is serious business and takes full concentration of the driver. If requests to passengers to quit fooling around and settle down go unheeded, pull over onto the nearest shoulder and wait until the passengers abide by your wishes. Then proceed on your way.

Safety Seat Rules of Thumb

- ❏ Always use child-safety seats and/or safety belts correctly.

- ❏ Restrain children ages 12 and under in a back seat.

- ❏ Follow child safety seat instruction manual and motor vehicle owner's manual for directions on proper installation.

- ❏ Restrain infants, until at least 1 year old and at least 20 pounds, in rear-facing child safety seats.

- ❏ Never put a rear-facing infant or convertible safety seat in the front passenger seat of a vehicle with an active passenger air bag.

- ❏ Children more than 1 year old, weighing 20 to 40 pounds, should be placed in forward-facing child-safety seats.

- ❏ Children 4 to 8 years old, weighing 40 to 80 pounds, should be placed in a car booster seat and restrained with a lap/shoulder belt every time they ride.

To reduce accidents, advises the American Academy of Pediatrics, child restraint devices or CRDs, must be appropriate for the particular vehicle's seat and seat belt, and the child's age and weight. CRDs must be positioned correctly, and used consistently. They must also meet or exceed federal motor vehicle standard 213 (FMVSS 213). Current guidelines are available from the National Center for Injury Prevention & Control. Child passenger protection laws exist in all 50 states. To review the law for your state, go to www.safekids.org. Under "Learn about child safety laws & regulations," select your state, and then select the topic "car."

Most organizations have found that the 12-passenger van is preferable to the 16-passenger van because it's closer in size to the vehicles usually operated by volunteer drivers, and it doesn't require a special license.

According to the National Highway Traffic Safety Administration, all 50 states, the District of Columbia, Puerto Rico, and the U.S. Territories have child passenger safety ("car seat") laws. Most, if not all, permit police officers to stop vehicles and issue citations solely for violations of child restraint laws.

Pedestrian

Children younger than 8 years are not physically, behaviorally or cognitively able to be safe pedestrians. Peripheral vision, depth perception, stature, and inability to concentrate on multiple activities all work against their success. Children are impulsive and have difficulty judging speed, spatial relations, distance and velocity, according to National SAFE KIDS campaign. Not until age 10 are children's hearing and sight, depth perception and scanning ability mature enough for them to handle traffic threats on their own. No matter how adept the child seems, adult supervision is needed for walking to and from home, to the playground, to your facility or when playing near streets.

Although deaths from pedestrian injuries have decreased because children are walking less, it remains the third leading cause of unintentional injury-related death among children ages 5 to 14, according to statistics reported by National SAFE KIDS campaign. Children from birth to 2 years old are more at risk from nontraffic-related pedestrian injuries — those that occur in driveways and parking lots — more than half which happen when vehicles are backing up.

<table>
<tr><td colspan="2">Safety Seat Recalls or Notices</td></tr>
</table>

Safety Seat Recalls or Notices

To ask about child safety seat product recalls or safety notices, call the National Highway Traffic Safety Administration's Auto Safety Hotline at (888) 327-4263.

Street Risks for Children

Children 14 and under are more likely to suffer pedestrian injuries if the area has:

❑ high traffic volume
❑ high number of parked cars
❑ higher posted speed limits
❑ undivided highway
❑ fewer stop lights, stop signs, crossing guards, and
❑ few alternative areas to play.

Adapted from National SAFE KIDS Campaign Web site.

Risk Management Strategies

To protect youth in your care, teach caregivers the Do's and Don'ts of pedestrian safety. The most important thing they can do to protect children in their care is to demonstrate and teach safe pedestrian behavior. Caregivers should always cross streets at the corner using crosswalks, look left and right and then left again, make eye contact with the driver before crossing, and obey the "WALK" and "DON'T WALK" lights. Children under 10 shouldn't ever be allowed to cross a street without adult supervision while in the care of your nonprofit. Organizations should also be alert to the possibility of impulsivity on the part of children, such as dashing out into the street to retrieve an errant baseball without pausing to check for traffic.

Children aren't the only ones who are impaired when it comes to traffic. Drivers are distracted by technology: wireless phones, radios, CDs, computers, faxes are all vying for attention the driver used to apply to the road. Help children protect themselves around traffic. Children shouldn't:

❑ run into the street; if a ball needs to be retrieved, ask an adult to get it.

❑ cross in the middle of the block or from between parked vehicles; drivers don't expect them there and can't see younger children.

❑ play in driveways, streets, parking lots or unfenced yards next to streets.

If there aren't any sidewalks, walk facing traffic, as far to the left as possible.

Teach Street Smarts

❑ Cross at the corner.

❑ Use crosswalks.

❑ Look left and right and left again.

❑ Make eye contact with driver before crossing.

❑ Obey traffic signals.

Bicycles

Head injury is the leading cause of death and permanent injury in bicycle crashes, according to the National SAFE KIDS Campaign. An estimated 500 bicycle-related fatalities and 151,000 nonfatal head injuries could be prevented each year if every rider wore a helmet, according to an article published in the *Journal of the American Medical Association* in 1996. That's one less death per day and one less injury every four minutes. An article in *Injury Prevention* in 1996 estimated that bicycle helmets are worn 25 percent of the time by children 5 to 14 years old and that teens hardly ever wear them. By 2010, the Public Health Services of the U.S. Department of Health and Human Services aims to have 50 percent of 9th to 12th graders wearing bicycle helmets. Thus you'll be receiving compliance help from national campaigns, and state and local legislation. For a current summary of mandatory state and local helmet laws, logon to the Bicycle Helmet Safety Institute Web site (www.bhsi.org).

4 "S"s of Helmet Choice

1. **Sticker** — Says helmet conforms to 1999 U.S. Consumer Product Safety Commission federal safety standard.

2. **Size** — Fits child comfortably and snugly, but not too tightly; add foam pads to ensure snug fit.

3. **Straight** — Sits on top of the head, in a level position and doesn't rock back and forth or side to side.

4. **Straps** — Adjust them according to manufacturer's directions to ensure the helmet stays on during impact.

(Adapted from Injury Prevention and Control for Children and Youth, pages 14-15, and "Preventing Bicycle-related Head Injuries" at www.cdc.gov/ncipc/factsheets/bikehle.htm)

Children need to know and obey the bicycle rules of the road. In addition, children shouldn't ride in the street until they are 10 years old and know and agree to obey the traffic laws.

Bicycle Injury Prevention

- Wear a Helmet.

- Make it cool: everybody do it.

- Make it a tool: strap on your helmet before mounting your bike.

- Make it a rule: dismount your bike, take off your helmet.

Obey the Traffic Laws

- Ride with traffic.

- Stay on the right.

- Use hand signals.

- Respect traffic signs and lights.

- Look both ways.

Scooters

For the first time in September 2000, reports the Consumer Product Safety Commission, scooter injuries surpassed in-line skating injuries. That month alone there were 8,600 injuries; nearly one-third happened to children younger than 8 years old, as reported by the AAA Foundation for Traffic

Safety, which says proper use of helmets could reduce brain injuries by 85 percent. The Brain Injury Association says that "brain injuries can be particularly serious in children, whose heads are proportionately larger than adults," which causes them to land head first.

Risk Management Strategies

Children younger than 8 years old shouldn't ride scooters without close adult supervision, according to the Consumer Product Safety Commission. The CPSC also recommends wearing a bicycle helmet, kneepads and elbow pads, similar to the advice it gives for in-line skating injury prevention. In-line skate helmets and bicycle helmets are designed to meet the same American Society for Testing and Materials standard and will protect scooter riders, as well.

Drowning

Drowning is the second leading cause of unintentional injury-related death in children ages 14 and under. The majority of drowning and near-drowning incidents occur in home swimming pools and in open water. Because children can drown in as little as one inch of water, they are at risk in wading pools, bathtubs, buckets, diaper pails, toilets and decorative ponds. The majority of children who survive are found within two minutes of submerging, according to the National SAFE KIDS Campaign.

A child's risk of drowning is related to its developmental stage and its environment. An infant is most likely to drown in a water-filled tub or bucket. Preschoolers are at greatest risk around swimming pools and spas. School-age children and teens are most likely to drown in natural bodies of water: lakes, ponds, streams, rivers, and swimming pools. Teenagers are also most likely to drown in natural bodies of water, and young men are much more at-risk than young women of this age group. Similar to motor vehicle accidents, risk-taking behavior and alcohol exacerbate the situation.

In addition to drowning deaths while swimming, children are at risk of drowning while diving, boating, and water or jet skiing. Children of all ages with seizure disorders are at greater risk of drowning than other children are.

Risk Management Strategies

To reduce the risk of injury, teach kids to respect water, to swim in pairs, to swim near a lifeguard station and to wear a personal flotation device or PFD when boating. The U.S. Coast Guard rates PFDs. Provide continuous adult supervision of infants while swimming, playing or bathing in water. Make certain liquid-filled containers (especially 5-gallon industrial ones) aren't left unsupervised around young children; be sure to empty containers and turn them up-side-down when the job is done. Swimming pools and decorative ponds are "attractive nuisances" under law. To protect children and your nonprofit from harm, surround them with a minimum four-foot-high fence, and include a self-closing and self-latching gate; keep the fence and gate maintained. Always have appropriate supervision of aquatic program areas. Monitor the performance of lifeguards to ensure that when on duty their attention is focused on what's happening in the water and not on homework or trying to get a date with an attractive participant. Teach children proper use of water sports equipment, as well as safety rules for boating, skiing and diving.

Open water poses additional risks. Listen to weather reports before venturing forth to swim or boat. Thunderstorms and strong winds can be extremely dangerous to both. Make certain people swim within designated areas, usually marked by buoys or ropes. Always provide and make certain everyone uses U.S. Coast Guard-approved life jackets when boating, no matter how short the trip or how accomplished the swimmer. Study the current and rip tides before embarking into unfamiliar waters. Canoes, kayaks and white-water rafts allow access to the "lure of the wild." Make certain that participants travel with knowledgeable guides, wear safety gear and carry emergency provisions.

Water Safety Guidelines for Caregivers

For Infants and Preschoolers

- ❑ *Never* leave a child unsupervised in or around water.
- ❑ Provide constant, direct supervision of young children around any bodies/containers of water.
- ❑ Supervise children in the water even if they are wearing personal flotation devices.
- ❑ Always remove pool cover completely.
- ❑ Remove and secure steps to above-ground pools when they aren't in use.
- ❑ Train one or more staff or volunteers in CPR and keep rescue equipment poolside: life preserver, shepherd's crook and wireless phone.
- ❑ Instruct staff and volunteers fully about pool, tub and bucket safety.

For School-age Children

- ❑ If program involves swimming or water sports, ensure that children learn to swim from qualified instructors who incorporate safety training into the lessons.
- ❑ Supervise all recreational swimming by a lifeguard or adult who can swim.
- ❑ Train one or more staff or volunteers in CPR and keep rescue equipment poolside: life preserver, shepherd's crook and wireless phone.
- ❑ Provide Coast Guard-approved personal flotation devices or PFDs and make sure children wear them during recreational boating, rafting, water-skiing and other water sports.

continued on next page

❑ Teach diving safety; Red Cross recommends minimum of 9 feet unobstructed water.

❑ Teach children pool slide safety: go down feet-first only.

For Teenagers

❑ Advise teens to always swim with at least one other person.

❑ Teach teens diving safety: no alcohol, no diving in shallow water (or water where there might be rocks or underwater hazards), and no diving in aboveground pools or off piers or docks. They should only dive from end of pool's diving board. If they jump from the side, they should go in feet first.

❑ Teach teens CPR or arrange for instruction.

Adapted from *Injury Prevention and Control for Children and Youth*, pages 229-230, and National Center for Injury Prevention & Control fact sheets.

Scalds, Burns and Fires

The age and developmental level of the child affects the type of injury from a scald or burn. Children age 4 and younger and children with disabilities are at the greatest risk for injury. Because young children have thinner skin, theirs burns at lower temperatures and more deeply than older children's does. They are especially at risk from scald and contact burns. Infants can be scalded when drinking liquids or eating foods heated in a microwave, by steam or being bathed in water that's too hot or hasn't been properly mixed. Toddlers may be burned by spilled hot food or beverages, or by touching hot surfaces or electrical wiring. Young school-age children play with matches or cigarette lighters and can catch their clothes on fire or burn their fingers. Adolescents in their risk-taking stage may be burned in all these ways plus by lighted tobacco products, fireworks, chemicals, electricity, faulty wiring or flammable liquids.

Leave fireworks displays to trained professionals, says the National Center for Injury Prevention & Control. That's the best way to prevent injury. Curiosity, lack of physical coordination and lack of supervision cause damage to hands and fingers, head and face, and eyes. The 4th of July and New Year's Eve may entice children, especially boys between 10 and 14, to purchase firecrackers, bottle rockets and sparklers to set off in your parking lot. In addition to burning the participants and bystanders, there is a risk of setting your property on fire.

Risk Management Strategies

Fire extinguishers required by the fire code must be inspected each year. Properly used, a fire extinguisher can save lives. But using the wrong type of extinguisher on a fire can actually spread the fire. Your main concern is the safety of the youth in your care, your staff and volunteers. No one should put himself at risk to extinguish a fire; that's the fire department's job. However, some small fires can be contained safely. Removing the oxygen from a grease fire by putting the lid on the pan, or smothering the flames with table salt, when it can be done safely, can solve the problem.

Some local ordinances or building codes require anti-scald plumbing devices on new construction. Many state laws require smoke alarms be used in new and existing dwellings. Check the applicable code in your community to make certain that your nonprofit is in compliance.

Tips to Lessen Burn Injuries

❑ Keep matches and lighters out-of-sight and away from children's reach.

❑ Teach employees, volunteers, clients to "stop, drop and roll" (burning clothes).

❑ Hold fire drills on a regular basis.

❑ Install fire extinguishers at logical sites (near kitchens and other sources of heat or flames); make certain they are the correct type; inspect and replace on regular basis; train staff to use them; only people trained to use extinguishers should use them on a fire.

❑ Install smoke alarms [the CDC suggests ones with lithium-powered batteries (that can last up to 10 years) and hush buttons]; replace batteries in smoke alarms with regular batteries once a year.

❑ Test smoke alarms monthly.

❑ Store flammable liquids (gasoline, acetone, turpentine, alcohol, benzene, charcoal lighter fluids, paint and lacquer thinner and contact cement) properly labeled in a tightly closed safety can that is outside, out of reach of children and far away from ignition sources (gas water heater pilot light).

❑ When replacing furnishings look for fire-resistant or fire-retardant materials.

❑ Maintain water heater temperature at 120°F.

❑ Have a designated smoking area with proper ashtrays for staff and visitors who must smoke. Police the area of litter, keep ashtray emptied.

❑ Cover radiators (don't use metal). Space heaters should not be used.

❑ Don't use halogen lamps in areas with children (bulbs get very, *very* hot).

Adapted from *Injury Prevention and Control for Children and Youth*, pages 239-240, and National Center for Injury Prevention & Control fact sheets.

Carbon Monoxide

CO, often called the "senseless" killer, is a colorless, odorless, tasteless gas that can cause headaches, dizziness, nausea, faintness and, at high levels, death. The American Lung Association reports exposures especially affect unborn babies, infants and people with anemia or a history of heart or respiratory disease.

According to the Environmental Protection Agency, sources of carbon monoxide are unvented kerosene and gas space heaters; leaking chimneys and furnaces; back-drafting from furnaces, gas water heaters, wood stoves and fireplaces; gas stoves; automobile exhaust from attached garages; and environmental tobacco smoke.

At low concentrations, symptoms of CO exposure include: fatigue in healthy people and chest pain in people with heart disease. At higher concentrations — impaired vision and coordination; headaches; dizziness; confusion; nausea. CO exposure can cause flu-like symptoms (headaches, tightness of chest, dizziness fatigue, confusion and breathing difficulties, and a pinkish or reddish tinge to the skin from elevated blood pressure) that clear up after leaving the building. CO exposure can be fatal at very high concentrations (such as being in an enclosed garage when the vehicle's motor is running).

Underwriters Laboratory lists signs of a CO problem on its Web site, www.ul.com/consumers. These include:

- streaks of carbon or soot around the service door of your fuel-burning appliances;

- the absence of a draft in your chimney;

- excessive rusting on flue pipes or appliance jackets;

- moisture collecting on the windows and walls of furnace rooms;

- fallen soot from the fireplace;

- small amounts of water leaking from the base of the chimney;

- damaged or discolored bricks at the top of your chimney; and

- rust on the portion of the vent pipe visible from outside the building.

UL recommends you place a UL Listed CO detector outside sleeping areas (nap rooms, dormitories in residential facilities). These detectors will sound an alarm before CO accumulates at dangerous levels. CO indicator cards and other devices detect elevated levels of CO but most don't sound an alarm to wake you at night when most CO poisonings occur. UL advises you to read the manufacturer's directions carefully. Don't install within five feet of chemicals. Monthly tests are advised for units wired directly into the building's electrical systems. Weekly tests and annual battery replacement are recommended for battery operated units.

If the alarm sounds, indicating elevated levels of CO, immediately open doors and windows. (If CO poisoning symptoms are exhibited by anyone, get everyone out and call the fire department.) Turn off fuel-burning appliances and call a qualified technician to find the source of the CO and repair it. Don't run any fuel-burning appliances until this is complete. Always heed the alarm and take action.

Risk Management Strategies

This is a compilation of advice offered by the American Lung Association, the U.S. Fire Administration's Office of Fire Management Programs and the Environmental Protection Agency.

❑ Make sure gas and other fuel-burning appliances are installed and working according to manufacturer's instructions and building codes.

❑ Have only a qualified technician install or convert fuel-burning equipment from one type to another.

❑ Use the manufacturer's recommended fuel in kerosene space heaters and only use them in well-ventilated rooms. (Note: Be aware that space heater use can increase burn injuries.)

❑ Install and use an exhaust fan vented to outdoors over gas stoves.

❑ Don't use ovens and gas ranges to heat the building.

❑ Open flues when fireplaces are in use.

❑ Choose properly sized wood stoves that are certified to meet EPA emission standards. Make certain that doors on all wood stoves fit tightly.

❑ Have a trained professional inspect, clean and tune-up central heating system (furnaces, flues and chimneys) annually. The water heater and stove should also be inspected yearly. Repair any leaks right away.

❑ Don't idle vehicles inside a closed garage.

❑ Don't burn charcoal or use charcoal grills inside a building, cabin, tent, camper or unventilated garage.

❑ Install a UL Listed CO detector, following manufacturer's instructions, outside sleeping areas, but not across from fuel-burning appliances.

❑ Educate staff to be alert to the danger signs that signal a CO problem and how to respond to a CO detector's alarm.

Choking, Strangulation and Suffocation

By four months old, infants are able to *bring* objects to their mouths. By six months old, they can pick up small objects and *put them in* their mouths. When nearing one year old, children can pull themselves up on furniture, which can fall on them; or toy boxes, whose lids can close on them; reach for and put cords around their necks; and play with plastic bags, which they can inhale.

Children younger than three years old have difficulty eating food that requires a lot of chewing to digest, and their ability to swallow develops at different rates. Children who put everything into their mouths—and those who eat while rushing, running or laughing—are at greatest risk of choking.

Any object small enough to fit in a child's mouth is a hazard. Ones that could lodge in the esophagus are even more so. A penny is a perfect example of an object of dangerous size and shape to a child. Other problem objects are parts of toys designed for older children, jewelry, arts and crafts items, small pieces of hardware, office supplies, small rubber balls and marbles.

The threat of suffocation may be apparent for younger children, but adolescents who are testing boundaries and independence are also at risk. The U.S. Coast Guard warns "teak/drag surfing" is a phenomenon that's gaining momentum and causing death by carbon monoxide asphyxiation. This surfing can only be done alone, the person can't wear a life vest and the "joy" of body surfing in a boat's wake puts the person directly behind the exhaust and in danger of being swept into the boat's propellers. Thus, watch for anyone grabbing the swim platform of a vessel while it's under way.

Risk Management Strategies

You need to make certain that caregivers supervise mealtimes, and prepare and cut food for young children. Caregivers should teach children to eat while sitting at a table, and to chew food well before swallowing.

Young children should only have access to age-appropriate toys. This means play areas need to be segregated and toys for young children need to be stored separately. All toys need to be checked frequently for sharp edges; damaged toys need to be repaired or replaced. Preferably, toy boxes should be lidless or have lightweight lids that lift off and can be set aside during playtime. Toy boxes with lids should have ventilation holes to prevent suffocation should a child be trapped inside. Latex balloons should be given only to children 8 years and older. If young children are around balloons, they must be supervised. It only takes a minute for an older child's popped balloon piece to be grabbed and ingested by a toddler.

To avoid strangulation, remove hood or neck drawstrings from children's clothing, and don't hang pacifiers around infants' necks. Infants, especially, are at risk of getting their heads caught between objects and being unable to extricate themselves. Be sure that openings in cribs, playground equipment, strollers, carriages and high chairs that can entrap infants' heads

Small Round Foods Can Cause Choking

While these foods may be consumed on a regular basis in the home, if your nonprofit serves children under 6 years old, you may wish to prohibit these foods from your meal service. Remember to keep children seated while they eat and always supervise mealtimes.

Not advised for children under age 6

- ❑ hot dogs
- ❑ sausages
- ❑ grapes
- ❑ carrots
- ❑ peanuts
- ❑ seeds from fruits or vegetables
- ❑ candies
- ❑ popcorn

meet suggested standards. Tie up window blind or drapery cords, which can become nooses if left free. Direct young children and teach older children to remove their bicycle helmets before climbing trees or playing on playground equipment.

Poison

Child-resistant packaging, product reformulation, parent awareness, and appropriate physician and poison control centers responses have reduced the death rate from poisoning in children ages 14 and younger, yet they are still at greater risk than adults of being poisoned. They're smaller, have faster metabolic rates and are less physically able to handle toxic substances, reports National SAFE KIDS Campaign.

More than 90 percent of childhood poisonings happen in the home, but you don't want your nonprofit to be included in the 10 percent that aren't. The culprits are medicine, household products, plants, lead and carbon monoxide. Among children ages 5 and younger, 40 percent are by medicines and 60 percent are by cosmetics, cleaning substances, plants, foreign objects and toys, pesticides, art supplies and alcohol. This same group is at risk from ingesting dust or chips from deteriorating lead-based paint. Carbon monoxide poisoning is most common during the winter months from unvented auxiliary heaters.

The American Academy of Pediatrics says poison ingestion is unintentional among almost all preschoolers and 90 percent of grade-school children. Among teenagers 50 percent is unintentional; the intentional half is related to suicide attempts or gestures and substance abuse. See Chapter 8 on Health Related Risks for more on these teen issues.

As mobility increases and adult supervision lessens, reports the AAP, toddlers and preschool children are more at risk. Their curiosity and inability to understand the associated dangers exacerbate the situation. School-age children understand the dangers and develop self-control, but still should be monitored when taking medication. The teen years tilt the scales. Suicide, recreational drugs, peer pressure and boundary testing all contribute to the 50:50 ratio of intentional versus unintentional poisoning.

Risk Management Strategies

Lock medications and diluted cleaning solutions in cabinets or file boxes. Don't allow concentrated solutions to be kept in the classroom or playroom. Make certain that trashcans are covered and secured. Instruct the cleaning crew to empty buckets of cleaning solution, rinse them with clear water and put them away immediately after use.

Clear poisonous plants from the area surrounding the playground. Store kitchen, bathroom and classroom cleaning supplies in their own locked

Emergency Phone Numbers

- Poison Center (call first)

- Emergency medical service

- Emergency department

- Pediatric inpatient services

storage unit. Only allow nontoxic art supplies, such as natural dyes and water-based products, to be used. Avoid aerosol sprays and solvent-based glues.

Check with your poison control center to see if they recommend that you keep syrup of ipecac and/or charcoal in your nonprofit's first aid supplies to help reduce the effects of unintentional poisoning. Ask how they recommend them to be used and for which specific poisons. Keep a list of emergency phone numbers visible by each phone.

Dr. Alan Woolf, president of the American Association of Poison Control Centers says, "When you call your poison control center, you will get immediate help from specially trained nurses, pharmacists and physicians 24 hours a day, 7 days a week." These experts "will tell you exactly what to do at the time that you call. If you need hands-on medical care, the poison center staff will provide the up-to-date treatment information about the poisoning to paramedics, nurses and physicians in the emergency department and to the patient's own doctor."

Animals

Whether or not your program includes pets, teaching children about pet treatment will help protect them from injury. As with other risks of injury, the younger the child, the more supervision that's required. When a child younger than five plays with a pet, the pet can get peeved and go into a defensive mode. A child this young can't read the signs that an older child or adult can. As children age, they spend more and more time away from home in child-care settings, schools, camps, and after-school youth or sports programs. Simple safety rules will help protect them and your nonprofit.

Kids With Pets

- ❏ Avoid all animals you don't know, especially ones who are wild or appear sick.

- ❏ Never break up a fight between animals.

- ❏ Always speak to an animal as you approach so it knows you're there; don't sneak up on it.

- ❏ When an animal is eating or sleeping, leave it alone.

- ❏ Never tease an animal, pull its tail, or take away its bone, food or toy.

- ❏ Never hold an animal close to your face.

- ❏ Respect animals; never intentionally hurt them.

Injury by Site

In addition to causes of accidents and injuries there are sites where certain accidents and injuries are most bound to occur.

Home

Home is the most dangerous place for children younger than 15 years old, especially preschool children, in terms of nonfatal and fatal injuries. The most common causes of fatal injuries in this age group are suffocation, fires and burns, and drowning. Falls are the leading cause of nonfatal home injury.

Risk Management Strategies

Although *The Season of Hope* focuses on nonprofits, many of the same safety precautions identified in this book for youth-serving organizations can be employed in the home. Fact sheets produced by the National Safety Council and the Consumer Product Safety Commission listed in the resource section of this book are helpful to parents.

Schools

Between ages 5 and 18, children spend more than 1,000 hours per year in school—most of their waking lives, according to the article "The epidemiology of nonfatal injuries among U.S. children and youth," in the *American Journal of Public Health*. Ten to 20 percent of the school-age children's injuries occur in school. The AJPH article goes on to say that more than one-third of the injuries are related to sports and recreational activities and nearly one-third from falls during other activities. Risks vary by age group: elementary students are more vulnerable on the playground, middle school students in the gym and high school students on the playing field, according to a 1992 article in the *American Journal of Preventative Medicine*. More than 2 million injuries requiring medical attention occur in schools annually.

Upper level science classes, industrial arts classes and arts classes using toxic, flammable or explosive products require running water, fire extinguishers, smoke detectors as well as protective eye-wear and aprons.

Concerns about students who bring weapons to school to harm other students and/or teachers are dealt with in Chapter 5.

Risk Management Strategies

Risk management strategies include training school staff in emergency first aid and CPR, regularly maintaining equipment and facilities, making certain safety equipment is maintained and regularly used in all sports activities, and matching children according to skill level, weight and physical maturity especially for contact sports. Teach children to remain seated on the school bus, exit the bus by the front door and cross the street 10 feet in front of the bus, in order to avoid the driver's blind spot.

Summer Camps

More than 5 million children attend summer camps annually. They include day camps, overnight camps, wilderness camps, and camps for children with special needs. The challenge is to provide safe, valuable experiences while minimizing risks from flora and fauna, sports and recreational activities.

Risk Management Strategies

Every camp needs policies and procedures to ensure the health and safety of the campers and the staff. Include procedures for record keeping, administering medications, and training staff to give first aid and basic life support. Have a system for reporting, recording treating and following up on minor injuries; requirements for using protective equipment; and emergency trauma plans (access to medical resources and parental notification).

Inspect campgrounds and buildings and maintain them in good repair to avoid injury and accidents. Safety and quality of food and water, and the potential for food-borne illnesses must be considered. Calculate exposure to poisonous berries and vegetation, excessive heat and sun, animals and insects that can cause trauma, infectious disease or toxic reactions in to your activities. Plan how to educate campers and provide antidotes for camp counselors and counselors in training to use if the worst case scenarios play out.

Other considerations are the training and supervision of camp staff, consequences caused by the lack of full parental disclosure of the child's health and behavioral history, and the increased number of children with chronic illnesses, medication needs or disabilities who are attending camp. A source for information on camp safety is the American Camping Association, www.acacamps.org.

Playgrounds

Playground injuries are the leading cause of injury in the child-care setting and to children ages 5 to 14 years in the school setting. Each year more than 200,000 children go to U.S. hospital emergency rooms with injuries associated with playground equipment, reports the U.S. Consumer Product Safety Commission. Most of these injuries are from falls to the surface surrounding equipment or onto equipment itself.

Falls account for the greatest number (75 percent) and most severe damage to children on playgrounds. Slides, swings and climbing equipment are the usual culprits. Severity of injury depends on the height of the fall, the position of the child's body when it hits the ground and the surface on which the child lands. Fractures cause the most severe head injury.

Risk Management Strategies

There are several strategies that will help protect children from playground injuries and death. These include design and layout of playground equipment, regular maintenance, timely repair of equipment, and careful supervision of children at play.

To reduce injuries from falls, the total area under and surrounding the playground equipment must be properly cushioned with an energy-absorbing surface. This area is called the "fall zone." As stated on page 75, the Consumer Product Safety Safety Commission's standards for cushioning material is a depth of at least 12 inches and a radius of at least six feet. The radius of the area increases in proportion to the height of the equipment. The greater the fall, the more damage can occur to the child. The CPSC publishes formulas for calculating adequate fall zones. The Access Board lists Americans with Disabilities Act, *Accessibility Guidelines for Play Areas* at (www.access-board.gov). In addition to providing proper cushioning material of the recommended depth and radius, the material must be maintained at the proper depth; kept clear of harmful debris such as glass, rocks and cans; and cleared of tree roots.

Another design consideration is the amount of room needed to protect the child exiting from a piece of equipment. There should be adequate "clear area" between play zones and hazards to keep the child exiting a piece of equipment from colliding with other children, or walls, asphalt walks and other play equipment. Play structures more than 30 inches high should be a minimum of 9 feet apart, advises the Consumer Product Safety Commission.

The playground should be designed to allow the teacher or playground supervisor to view the entire playground at once. Consider the topography of the site; make sure that natural contours don't cause barriers. Consider how pieces of play equipment relate to one another; make certain that large ones don't impede vision of those smaller pieces. Landscaping plans need to take into account the small stature of the participants and not impede sight lines of caregivers.

When possible, the playground should be enclosed with a fence a minimum of four feet high to keep children within the safe area you've created and make supervised play easier. Locate gates away from streets, and inspect the fence for defects such as jagged or protruding parts.

Each type of playground equipment has its own risks and special precautions. Climbing equipment accounts for almost 1/3 of all injuries.

Swings account for 1/4 of playground injuries. Slides, merry-go-rounds, teeter totters and spring rockers all require firm mounting in concrete, cushioned surface and inspection for worn, jagged or sharp edges.

Preschoolers require close supervision; older children require someone to "referee" so they don't misuse equipment, overcrowd or rough house.

All equipment must be regularly inspected for safety and scheduled for maintenance. Equipment should meet safety standards recommended by the American Society for Testing and Materials, U.S. Consumer Product Safety Commission, or the Consumer Federation of America.

Public Playground Safety Checklist

1. Make sure surfaces around playground equipment have at least 12 inches of wood chips, mulch, sand or pea gravel, or have mats made of safety-tested rubber or rubber-like mats.

2. Check that protective surfacing extends at least six feet in all directions from play equipment. For swings, be sure surfacing extends, in back and front, twice the height of the suspending bar.

3. Make sure play structures more than 30 inches high are spaced at least 9 feet apart.

4. Check for dangerous hardware, such as open "S" hooks or protruding bolt ends.

5. Make sure spaces that could trap children, such as openings in guardrails or between ladder rungs, measure less than 3.5 inches or more than 9 inches.

6. Check for sharp points or edges in equipment.

7. Look out for tripping hazards, like exposed concrete footings, tree stumps and rocks.

8. Make sure elevated surfaces, like platforms and ramps, have guardrails to prevent falls.

9. Inspect playgrounds regularly to see that equipment and surfacing are in good condition.

10. Carefully supervise children on playgrounds to make sure they're safe.

www.cpsc.gov/kids/kidsafety/plgdlist.pdf

Child-play Safety

Supervisors should make certain that:

- ❏ children under five play in separate area on age-appropriate equipment.

- ❏ children in their charge can always be seen and heard.

- ❏ children are prevented from pushing, shoving, crowding and using equipment inappropriately.

- ❏ children don't wear necklaces, purses, scarves or clothing with drawstrings while on playgrounds.

Factors Related to Playground Injury

- ❏ ground surface material

- ❏ safety gates

- ❏ swings

- ❏ mixed-age play

- ❏ young children using advanced equipment

- ❏ falls from equipment

- ❏ entrapment on equipment

Adapted from Injury Prevention and Control for Children and Youth *by the American Academy of Pediatrics.*

Sports

Organized sports and recreation can improve physical fitness, coordination, self-discipline and teamwork, but these beneficial activities put participants at risk for injury unless precautions are in place. Half of organized sports-related injuries are preventable, reports the National SAFE KIDS Campaign, "Injury Facts: Sports and Recreational Activity Injury" (www.safekids.org). It's a matter of protecting bodies while they are still growing and developing motor and cognitive skills.

Hospital emergency rooms treated an estimated 162,100 children just for baseball-related injuries, many of which were injuries to the head or face, according to the Consumer Product Safety Commission 1998 "Baseball Safety Factsheet." Most soccer injuries, on the other hand, occur to the lower extremities. Drs. David Barr and Roger Krause wrote in an article that first appeared in *Healthy Living News*, contusions, muscle strains and sprains of knees and ankles make up the majority of these injuries. Sports-related injuries occur more frequently in sports programs with higher levels of competition and then most often during practice rather than games.

The American Academy of Pediatrics says, "Injury rates are low for all sports at the youth level. Athletes prior to puberty don't generate enough force to cause a substantial number of injuries even in collision sports, such as football and ice hockey. Injury rates climb considerably when participants reach puberty and are substantial in youth of high school age and older."

Nonprofits that include sports and recreational activities in their programs need to take precautions to protect young athletes and the organization from harm. Whether they sponsor the activity directly or contract with another organization, it's your responsibility to see that youth in your program are safe from foreseeable harm. See sidebar for some risk management strategies.

Recreational Injuries

Children 5 to 14 years old account for nearly 40 percent of all sports-related injuries. In 1999, they were treated in hospital emergency rooms (doesn't include urgent care centers or doctor's offices) as follows:

Bicycle-related	340,000+
Playground equipment	208,000 (14 and under)
Trampoline	78,000 (14 and under)
Inline skating	58,600
Skateboarding	32,200
Roller skating	27,000
Unpowered scooter-related	26,000 (14 and under)
Snowboarding	19,000
Ice skating	16,000
Snow skiing	16,300
Sledding	14,000

Sports Injury Prevention Tips

❑ Dress participants in appropriate protective equipment.
❑ Maintain safe playing conditions.
❑ Enforce safety rules.
❑ Provide trained adult supervision of play.
❑ Match and group children according to skill level, weight and physical maturity.
❑ Provide proper training and skills building.
❑ Ensure children drink plenty of liquids while participating in athletic activities.

Adapted from Injury Facts *by National SAFE KIDS Campaign (www.safekids.org).*

Other Considerations

Weather

Weather causes a variety of injuries in children. Weather-related injuries include dehydration, hypothermia, heat stroke, electrocution by lightning, trauma due to wind blown debris, and frostbite. Thunderstorms and strong winds can be extremely dangerous to boaters and swimmers. Organizations with outdoor activities should keep an eye on weather conditions and respond accordingly, such as limiting activities when the weather is extreme — hot or cold. Staff should be trained to recognize and respond to the signs of weather-related conditions. Your policy might read: During electrical storms, get off the game field. Check the day's Air Quality Index. "Code Orange," indicates to keep children and adults with asthma and respiratory problems indoors. "Code Red" indicates to keep all children and adults indoors.

An Athlete Doesn't Need to Be Knocked Out to Have a Concussion

Which changes will you notice in the player's behavior?
- ❏ Inappropriate playing behavior (skating the wrong direction, shooting on own net)
- ❏ Significantly decreased playing ability from earlier in the game
- ❏ Being slow to answer questions or follow directions
- ❏ Being easily distracted
- ❏ Being unable to do normal activities
- ❏ Displaying unusual emotions (crying/laughing)
- ❏ Changes in personality
- ❏ Irritability and low frustration tolerance
- ❏ Anxiety and depressed mood
- ❏ Stare blankly
- ❏ Sleep disturbance

What will tell you that the player is unaware?
- ❏ Being unaware of time
- ❏ Being unaware of date
- ❏ Being unaware of place
- ❏ Being unaware of the period or score in the game
- ❏ Being generally confused

How will the player feel?
- ❏ Dazed, dinged or stunned
- ❏ Dizzy
- ❏ See stars or flashing lights
- ❏ Ears ringing
- ❏ Headache
- ❏ Sick or throwing up
- ❏ Blurred vision
- ❏ Poor coordination or balance
- ❏ Slurred speech

The presence of any of these symptoms can be a sign that an athlete has a concussion. Ask the player to sit down right away. Talk to the coach and have the child evaluated by a doctor.

Equipment Failure or Misuse

Safety equipment properly used and maintained reduces some kinds of risks, but when it's used improperly or worn out, its ability to protect is lost. For example, when a bicycle safety helmet is properly fitted and worn while riding a bike, it reduces the severity of a head injury if the biker falls off the bicycle. Children should be taught to remove their helmets when they get off their bicycles, because, although it seems that the helmet might protect them in other sorts of play where falls are prevalent, it can actually cause harm. According to the Consumer Product Safety Commission, several children have choked or received neck injuries when their bicycle safety helmets caught in the railings of playground equipment.

Likewise, climbing ropes, personal flotation devices, life-saving equipment for waterfront activities — all have limited life spans after which the equipment should be discarded or rendered useless for the original purpose, (i.e., old climbing ropes could be cut into pieces for jump-ropes). You must ensure that safety equipment isn't used beyond its useful life expectancy.

Trying to extend the life of what may be very expensive equipment would be a false economy and a big mistake, which would become immediately apparent should a child be seriously injured, or worse, die. Thus, safety equipment use may be the deciding factor in whether your organization can offer an outdoor activity such as white-water rafting, rock climbing or other high-adventure activities.

Familiarize your staff members with all of the safety equipment that they may be called upon to use in an emergency. This includes first aid equipment, building alarm systems and communications systems (PA systems, emergency radios, wireless phones, etc.).

Make sure that the vehicles (no matter who owns them or who drives them) used to transport your program's participants are maintained in good condition. Worn brake shoes, lack of rearview mirrors, rusted parts, and faulty axles are no excuse for an accident that injures or kills youth in your care or on your staff.

Teach safe practices to your employees, volunteers and program participants. Reduce dangerous behavior through modeling and demonstration. Document minor and major injuries in youth-serving organizations and programs to identify hazards and patterns then take corrective action. Establish policies and procedures to handle and report child injury. Inspect, maintain and replace equipment and premises. Set up a file system to keep reports on injuries and problems/solutions regarding equipment. Report any product hazards or product-related injuries to the U.S. Consumer Product Safety Commission at (800) 638-2772. Supervise closely those too young to care for themselves, and monitor the behavior or older, risk-taking adolescents.

Outfitting

To protect kids from bumps and bruises or more severe injury, participants in many types of activities need to be outfitted with proper equipment and clothing. These requirements have been part of the traditional health and safety requirements for many youth-serving organizations. This is simple risk management.

Organizations that permit youngsters to participate in activities despite inadequate equipment or without proper clothing may be responsible for child neglect. The neglect would be similar to parents who allow their children to go to school in freezing temperatures dressed only in summer clothing. To protect your program and its participants, clear policies on required preparations should be consistently enforced. A program may need to be canceled or a child kept out of the activity if they can't be properly outfitted.

The next chapter identifies three types of threats inherent in the newest risk management challenge to nonprofits: Internet use by children and youth. You can balance the benefits of this tool that's becoming integral to learning, and the risks of someone turning the tool on the learners and using it to harass or abuse them.

Chapter 7
Internet Access

To err is human — and to blame it on a computer is even more so.
　　　　　— Robert Orben

Computing is not about computers any more. It is about living.
　　　　　— Nicholas Negroponte

Access to the Internet is perhaps the newest risk management challenge related to the safety of young people in youth-serving organizations. This risk to organizations is too new to be able to quantify, and the incidents so far are more anecdotal than statistically significant. Many organizations ranging from summer camps to recreation centers now include computers in their programs. Many of these permit access to the Internet for participating children and teenagers. The availability of computers and access to the Internet is growing. Today, many letters from camp are e-mailed.

The anecdotal information available concerning dangers to children and youth on the Internet generally shows three kinds of threats in addition to the danger of allowing access to inappropriate materials that are found on the Internet. There is the threat of: 1) harassment, 2) stalking and 3) physical injury.

A recent nationwide survey of 1,501 10 through 17 year olds who use the Internet regularly confirmed that the Internet can be a potential source of danger for children. The findings of the survey, conducted by the University of New Hampshire's Crimes Against Children Research Center, include:

- Approximately one in five received a sexual solicitation or approach over the Internet in the last year.

- One in 33 received an aggressive sexual solicitation — a solicitor who asked to meet them somewhere, called them on the telephone, or sent them regular mail, money or gifts.

- One in four in the last year had an unwanted exposure to pictures of naked people or people engaged in sexual activities.

- One in 17 was threatened or harassed.

- Approximately 25 percent of young people who reported these incidents were distressed by them.

- Less than 10 percent of sexual solicitations and only 3 percent of unwanted exposure episodes were reported to authorities, such as a law-enforcement agency, an Internet service provider or a hotline.

- About 25 percent of the youth who encountered a sexual solicitation or approach told a parent. Almost 40 percent of those reporting an unwanted exposure to sexual material told a parent.

In addition to offering access to the Internet for young service recipients, most youth-serving organizations have Web sites. These sites range from simple "billboard" style sites containing only basic information about the organization, to more complex, interactive sites offering services, products and links. A disturbing number of these Web sites include information about individual children that may be sufficiently specific to identify particular children by name, street address, school, telephone number or e-mail address.

Tools for Managing the Risks of Internet Access

Many of the risks of Internet access can be avoided through establishing rules for using the Internet and giving orientation sessions to children before allowing them to use the Internet. The National Center for Missing and Exploited Children offers Internet safety materials suitable for use by children and teenagers available through the organization's Web site, www.missingkids.org.

Software filters can limit access to Internet materials that are unsuitable for young people. As with all software, these are being improved constantly. However, no software exists that can protect young people from unsavory individuals who resort to subterfuge and trickery for eliciting personal information from unwary children. These individuals may merely be gathering information to use in marketing products, but they may also be looking for children to sexually victimize. Education and supervised access are the keys to Internet safety for children.

Every youth-serving organization should consider taking the following steps to protect young service recipients:

❑ *Develop and distribute a Technology Policy or Acceptable Use Policy,* which establishes reasonable boundaries for acceptable use and provides examples of misuse in member/client guides, materials to parents and the Employee Handbook.

❑ *Refrain from featuring any information on the organization's Web site that could result in inappropriate access to young clients* (for example, listing children with their names, schools and/or e-mail addresses).

❑ *Invest in blocking/filtering software* to protect kids using the organization's computers from the seamier side of the Web. End-user solutions can block incoming information or e-mail and reside on the user's PC. Examples are Cyber Patrol, Cyber Snoop and Net Nanny. If serving children who are "computer literate and Internet savvy," layered protection may be in order. This would entail server-based blocking or limiting to child-friendly Web sites.

Nonprofits that provide Internet access to children should consider taking the following additional steps:

❑ *Provide an orientation or training session for children* who have access to the organization's computers covering the rules of use and what to do if someone solicits them over the Internet. For example, young clients of a nonprofit should be taught that:

■ Persons they meet online are strangers, no matter how friendly they appear to be.

■ They should never assume that an online correspondent is a young person — someone who claims to be a child could easily be an adult.

■ Personal information should never be shared online, nor should personal information be shared in an online profile.

■ They should never arrange to meet someone in person whom they have met online.

■ They should refrain from "flaming" (saying mean things about) other persons online.

■ They should follow the rules established by the Web sites or electronic lists they visit online.

■ They aren't allowed unlimited access to the Internet while participating in the organization's programs — time limits established by the organization must be adhered to.

■ Unmonitored access isn't provided — a staff member of the nonprofit may observe their online activity.

- They should immediately tell an adult when they receive disturbing or inappropriate messages, based on the content of the message or the possible age of the sender, using the software tools provided by the nonprofit for doing so.

- They may only use child-friendly search engines. Look on www.safekids.com/search.htm for a list of safe sites.

- Their access to the Internet will be restricted by content.

❏ *Establish an Acceptable Use Policy* for young clients, instruct young clients on the terms of the policy, and suspend access privileges for those who violate the policy.

❏ *Make certain that young clients know that they should have no expectation of privacy while using the organization's equipment to access the Internet.*

❏ *Establish a system for monitoring client use of the Internet.*

❏ *Place computers accessible by young clients in a central, not isolated, location.*

❏ *Periodically review the content of the organization's computers* to:

- Make certain that any of your organization's computers to which children have access don't contain inappropriate material or material appropriate for adult users only; and

- Look for downloaded images or programs.

❏ *Regularly review posted Web sites and links.* Since Web site content is subject to change, verify that the content is as acceptable as the day it was selected as appropriate for the program's participants.

❏ *Don't rely on software to prevent children from getting into trouble.* Use good supervision in conjunction with filtering software.

If Your Web Site Attracts Young Visitors

A growing percentage of youth-serving nonprofits operate Web sites. With millions of kids online every day, it may make good business sense to dedicate a portion of your site for young visitors. Any nonprofit that does so should keep in mind that special rules may apply. Organizations that operate Web sites or online services directed to children under 13 that collect personal information from children, or those that operate a general-audience Web site and have *actual knowledge* that they are collecting personal information from children, must comply with the *Children's Online Privacy Protection Act of 1998*. For key provisions of the Final Rule applying to COPPA, visit: www.ftc.gov/opa/1999/9910/childfinal.htm.

The rules or guidelines that should be presented in a training session should be adapted based on the age of an organization's participants. For young children, the following list of "Tips for Internet Safety and Good Manners" might be appropriate:

S A M P L E

Tips for Internet Safety and Good Manners

(Adapted from the list featured on the Kidscom.com Web site)

1. Always be polite and use good manners when talking to someone else online.

2. Ask your _____ (title of person supervising children at the nonprofit, such as counselor/team leader/coach, etc.) to spend time with you while online so that you can show them some of the neat things you can find online.

3. Only use the Internet when your _____ (title of person supervising children at the nonprofit, such as counselor/team leader/coach, etc.) tells you it's OK, and only for as long as you are supposed to.

4. Don't give out personal information such as your name, address, telephone number or school name to anyone unless you have permission from your parents.

5. Never meet with a cyber-friend unless your parents go with you or you have their permission to go alone.

6. Don't violate copyright law by taking words, pictures or sound from someone else's Web site without permission of the Web site owner.

7. Don't respond to any e-mail messages you get if they are strange, mean or upsetting to you, and tell your parents or teachers right away.

8. Don't send pictures of yourself or your family to anyone unless you have permission from your parents.

9. Stop right away if you see or read something on a Web site that upsets you and tell your parents, teachers or _____ (title of person supervising children at the nonprofit, such as counselor/team leader/coach, etc.) about it.

10. Don't put words, pictures or sounds on other people's Web sites without their permission.

Developing an Acceptable Use Policy

A connection to the Internet opens up endless opportunities for a youth-serving organization. In addition to harnessing the power of the Internet for the organization's own needs and purposes, a high-speed Internet connection can be a powerful educational tool.

Similar, yet different from employee policies, acceptable use policies for youth participants are just as important. One of the most important tools available to every youth-serving organization is a policy indicating the do's and don'ts of Internet access. Commonly called an "Acceptable Use Policy" or "AUP," this policy should describe permitted and prohibited uses of the organization's technology and makes it clear that a participant who violates the policy will lose access privileges. Nonprofits providing Internet access for young participants should always conduct an orientation before allowing clients to go online. The organization's Acceptable Use Policy should be described during this orientation.

Acceptable Use Policy Components Checklist

A well-written Acceptable Use Policy for a youth-serving nonprofit will generally include the following components:

❑ a statement on the educational uses of the Internet in the organization

❑ a list of the responsibilities of the organization's staff, participants and parents for using the Internet

❑ a code of conduct governing behavior on the Internet

❑ a description of the consequences of violating the AUP

❑ a description of what constitutes acceptable and unacceptable use of the Internet

❑ a statement reminding users that Internet access and the use of computer networks is a privilege

❑ a signature form for members/participants and parents indicating their intent to abide by the AUP.

School districts across the country have several years of experience using AUPs. Youth-serving nonprofits may want to adapt an AUP used in a local school district for their use. In the Norfolk (Va.) Public Schools, students must execute an *Internet Access Agreement* that includes three components:

1. confirms the student's agreement to abide by the school district's *Internet Use Procedure*,

2. certifies that the student has attended an Internet training session, and

3. includes a parent's signature granting permission for the account.

A copy of the Norfolk Internet Access Agreement is featured on the next page.

Norfolk Public Schools

Internet Access Agreement

Please fill out the form and submit it to the media specialist at your facility.

Acceptance of Internet Procedure

_____ understands and will obey the Norfolk Public Schools Internet Use Procedure. Any violation of this policy will result in the suspension of access privileges and may also be grounds for further disciplinary /legal action.

Signature _____ Date _____

Completion of Internet Training Session

_____ has completed a school-approved class that deals with the appropriate use of the Internet. This user is allowed to use the Internet for activities that are outlined in the Norfolk Public Schools Acceptable Internet Use Procedure.

User Signature/Date _____

School Official Signature/Date _____

Parent/Guardian/Sponsor (When Applicable)

As the parent/guardian/sponsor of this student, I have read the Norfolk Public Schools Internet Use Procedure. I understand that this access is to be used for approved educational purposes. I also recognize that it's impossible for Norfolk Public Schools to guarantee that my student won't gain access to controversial or inappropriate materials. Norfolk Public Schools will not be responsible for inappropriate material accessed on the Internet. Further, I accept full responsibility for supervision of my student's use of the Internet outside of the school setting. I give permission to issue an account to my student and certify that the information contained on this form is correct.

Parent/Guardian/Sponsor Name _____

Signature/Date _____

The Internet offers a world of knowledge and skill building for children and teens. The challenge for youth-serving organizations is to provide access to this wonderful tool while protecting the organization and its employees, volunteers and participants. Employment of sound risk management practices will provide that protection. Update your policies to include Internet use, train your staff, inform parents and let the young people in your programs know what is expected of them. Then monitor use and provide consequences for those who don't follow the guidelines.

The next chapter investigates physical and mental health problems that are brought into your nonprofit by young participants. Drugs and alcohol, which involve and affect both physical and mental health, are handled separately.

Chapter 8
Health Related Risks

Oh, for boyhood's painless play,
Sleep that wakes in laughing day,
Health that mocks the doctor's rules,
Knowledge never learned of schools.

— "The Barefoot Boy"
by John Greenleaf Whittier

When one child gets sick, the sports team, the Cub Scout pack, the day camp or nursery school class feels the effects. Whether it's a physical or mental illness there are repercussions for the rest of the children. The youth-serving nonprofit needs to have policies and procedures in place for when to send an ill child home, what to do if the parent or guardian is unavailable, what medicines staff can dispense and under what conditions, and what accommodations will be taken for an allergic or asthmatic child.

Physical Health

Children get sick. This is a fact that most organizations offering services to children and youth recognize. Some children have chronic conditions such as allergies and asthma; others merely have episodic illnesses such as the flu, measles or mumps. For organizations, the issue is what to do when a child becomes ill while participating in your program.

If the child's parents are present or reasonably available, the organization can turn the responsibility over to the parents for the medical care of the child. If the parents are not available, the organization must be prepared to render assistance to the child, as well as take reasonable steps to protect other children from contagion. Children who become ill while involved with your organization should be isolated from other children, to the extent possible, and made as comfortable as possible, while you're awaiting instructions from a physician or the child's parents.

Colds

According to the American Academy of Pediatrics, the common cold is really an upper respiratory infection that inflames the lining of the nose and throat. For five to 10 days children's noses may be runny or stuffy, and their eyes may be red and watery. They may sneeze, cough, experience aches and pains and have a mild fever.

There is a lot of misunderstanding about how colds are transmitted from child to child. Despite myths to the contrary, you can't catch colds from drafts, or from failing to wear a scarf or a heavy jacket in cool, wet weather. Colds are caused by viruses and are passed from one individual to another, usually through direct contact or by sharing objects such as utensils or handkerchiefs, as well as by coughs and sneezes. Colds are extremely contagious, particularly during the first day or two of the infection, when many of the symptoms may not yet be evident. Colds tend to be more prevalent in the fall and winter, when children are in school and are in closer contact with each other's cold viruses.

Generally, colds are self-limiting and disappear on their own without complications. Telephone the child's pediatrician if a youngster develops ear pain or a severe sore throat, has trouble breathing, or if the cold persists for more than 10 days or fever lasts longer than 48 hours. Children with colds may attend school and other activities, as long as they feel well enough to participate.

Vomiting and Diarrhea

Children who are vomiting or have diarrhea run the risk of becoming dehydrated. Only a physician can diagnose dehydration, but staff members can watch for some obvious signs: a dry mouth, no tears, sunken eyes, a reduction in urination and skin that stays compressed when pinched. Dehydration is a particularly serious problem for small children under five years of age.

The American Academy of Pediatrics recommends that for diarrhea with no dehydration, feed the child normally and give supplemental commercial rehydration fluids within four to six hours after a diarrheal episode. If the diarrhea persists, call the child's doctor. Plain liquids don't have the balance of minerals and salts that the body needs for proper functioning. For continuity of care, you should advise the parent of the occurrence(s).

According to the American Medical Association, some diarrheal infections pass from person to person on dirty hands. Dirty hands carry infectious germs into the body when children suck on their fingers, bite their nails, or put any part of their hands into their mouths. You can help prevent this by reminding the children in your program to keep their hands out of

---

Wash Away Infection

Staff can help to prevent the spread of infectious diseases by washing their hands frequently with soap and water and encouraging children to do the same.

their mouths (not to chew, bite or suck on their nails and fingers). Also remind them to wash their hands frequently, especially after using the toilet and before eating.

Food service practices are an important risk management consideration. To prevent diarrheal illness carried in contaminated food and water, wash fruits and vegetables thoroughly before eating. Also, wash kitchen counters and cooking utensils thoroughly after they have been in contact with raw meat, especially poultry. Refrigerate meats as soon as possible after purchase, and cook them until they are well done. Refrigerate cooked leftovers as soon as a meal is done — don't let them sit for hours on a kitchen counter.

If your program involves camping or hiking remind the children to never drink water from streams, springs or lakes unless local health authorities have certified that the water is pure enough for drinking. Also, be cautious when buying prepared foods from curbside vendors, especially if no local health agency oversees their operations.

Many youth-serving programs include animals in their programs. To prevent the spread of germs from the organization's pets, especially reptiles, keep pet feeding areas separate from areas where people eat. Never wash pet cages or bowls in the same sink used for food preparation. Insist that children wash their hands with soap and water after handling the animals.

Allergies and asthma

Allergic disorders rank first among children's chronic diseases. According to the American College of Allergy, Asthma and Immunology, any child may become allergic, but children from families with a history of allergy are more likely to be allergic. Children may inherit the tendency, but only some of them will develop active allergies. Allergic reactions show up in different ways. Some children develop skin rashes (atopic dermatitis), some develop asthma, and some get hay fever. The child with allergies may also have itchy, watery red eyes and chronic ear problems.

Allergic rhinitis, also known as hay fever, is the most common of all allergy problems. Its symptoms are a runny, itchy nose; sneezing; postnasal drip; and nasal congestion. Although "hay fever" is associated with late summer/early fall, allergic rhinitis can occur at any time of the year, be seasonal or be present year-round. The following are a few of the problems related to allergic rhinitis.

■ *Nasal Congestion* — Allergies are the most common cause of chronic nasal congestion in children. Sometimes a child's nose is congested (obstructed) to the point that breathing is only possible through the mouth, especially while sleeping.

■ *Ear Infections* — Allergies lead to inflammation in the ear and may cause fluid accumulation that can promote ear infections and decreased hearing. If this happens when the child is learning to talk, poor speech development may result. Clinically, allergies can cause earaches, as well as ear itching, popping and fullness ("stopped up ears"). Anyone with these symptoms should be considered for allergy testing and treatment.

At School and in Other Programs

For allergic children, closed environments related to school exacerbate problems of hay fever. These may cause absences due to the increased incidence of allergic episodes. The American College of Allergy, Asthma and Immunology identifies the following problems to look for so that an allergy can be properly diagnosed and treated, as well as several suggestions for helping the allergic child.

■ *Dust irritation.* Reducing exposure to dust will be helpful to most allergic children. At school, children with allergic problems should sit away from the blackboards to avoid irritation from chalk dust.

■ *Animals.* Dander, saliva and fur trigger reactions in allergic children. Furry animals may cause problems for allergic children. If the child has more problems while at school or at the youth center, it could be the program's pet.

■ *Asthma and physical education.* Physical education and sports are a big part of the day for many children. Having asthma doesn't mean eliminating these activities. Often medication administered by inhaler is prescribed before exercise to control symptoms. Children with asthma and allergies should be able to participate in any sport they choose — provided the doctor's advice is followed.

■ *Dry air.* With the onset of cold weather, using a humidifier to accompany forced air heating systems may be helpful in some regions of the country. Adding a small amount of moisture to dry air makes breathing easier for most people. Don't allow humidity to exceed 40 percent, or it will promote the growth of dust mites and mold, which trigger allergic reactions.

■ *Change in behavior.* Since children can't always verbally express their annoying or painful symptoms, they may exhibit behavior changes instead. Be on the alert for possible allergies if a child has bouts of irritability, temper tantrums or decreased ability to concentrate. These are all signs of "allergic irritability syndrome" often caused by nose, ear and sinus symptoms in allergic children. Sometimes allergic children become overactive, and usually, their schoolwork suffers. (attention deficit disorder isn't caused by allergies.) When a child's allergies are properly treated, his or her symptoms, behavior, and school performance can improve.

Organizations need to know how to respond in case of an allergic reaction or an asthma attack. To be prepared, take a careful medical history when a child is accepted into the program. Get parental permission to obtain medical care if the organization is unable to contact the parents, and prearrange access to emergency care from a nearby hospital emergency room or physician.

When it's necessary to take a child to the hospital emergency room, the staff should take the medical history and signed parental permission form with them. The information on the history form will be valuable to medical care providers and the permission form serves as documentation of your authority to seek medical assistance for the child.

With the emergence of AIDS as a health concern, universal precautions to prevent contact with bodily fluids have become the standard of care. This applies to the staff members caring for a sick or injured child or adolescent, as well as to other children in the program. First aid equipment should include latex gloves and plastic bags for disposal of contaminated wastes.

Head Lice

According to the American Medical Association, head lice infestations among children are generally caused by the head louse, *Pediculus humanus capitis*, a parasite about 2 to 4 mm long, which can be seen by the human eye. Head lice live among human hairs, feed on blood from the skin and lay eggs (called "nits") on hair shafts. Nits hatch within one week to two weeks after they are laid, and the newly hatched lice must bite and suck blood within 24 hours of hatching to survive. Louse bites may cause inflammation and itching, and they can become infected.

Head lice are passed from person to person in infested clothing, bed linens, combs, brushes and hats. They are spread by close personal contact between classmates and family members. Anyone can get head lice. Having head lice isn't a sign of poor hygiene. Even a daily bath or shower won't guarantee a "louse-proof" child. You can remind the children in your program to avoid using another person's comb, brush, towel or hat. You can also make sure that each child has his own personal comb and brush.

Some organizations have a "no nit" policy that prevents children who have visible nits from participating. Sometimes this policy includes children who have already received anti-lice treatments and whose remaining nits are dead. According to The American Academy of Pediatrics Committee on Infectious Disease, "no nit" policies haven't been shown to stop the spread of head lice. Organizations should consult their local department of public health or other health professionals to obtain guidance concerning effective organizational policies and practices for controlling this problem.

Too sick to participate?

Organizations need to establish policies that govern when a child is too sick to participate. Dr. Sandra Osborn, a pediatrician and past president of the State Medical Society of Wisconsin, says that fever is probably the most important factor to take into consideration. If the child's temperature is two degrees or more above his or her normal reading, that's a sign that medicine is necessary to bring down the fever. It's also a definite indication that school and other activities are out. Children who are ill need to stay home to recuperate, but also to avoid spreading the illness to their friends and adult leaders.

When children have a high fever they're mostly like to be contagious. Other key symptoms to watch for are cough, decreased appetite, vomiting, diarrhea, aches and pain. But don't feel shy about calling the doctor's office to ask for help if you're unsure. Nurses are very familiar with these symptoms and can give you a good idea whether it's necessary to send the child home or seek medical treatment.

Mental Health

An estimated 20 percent of American children and adolescents, 11 million in all, have serious diagnosable emotional or behavioral health disorders, which range from attention deficit disorder and depression to bipolar disorder and schizophrenia, according to research published by the Institute of Medicine. Between 9 and 13 percent of children ages 9 to 17 have serious mental or emotional disturbances that substantially interfere with or limit their ability to function in the family, school, and community, reports the Federal Register. It's estimated that between 43 and 70 percent of children in the child protection system have mental health problems severe enough to warrant intervention.

Since mental health issues are prevalent in our youth population, organizations offering services to children and youth need to be prepared to assist young people experiencing mental health problems and to protect them from harming themselves or other youth in their programs.

Depression

According to the American Psychiatric Association, as many as 10 percent of children between ages 6 and 12 experience persistent feelings of sadness — the hallmark of depression. Since children may not be able to understand or express many of the core symptoms that would indicate adult depression, parents should be aware of some key behaviors — in addition to changes in eating or sleeping patterns — that may signal depression in children:

- a sudden drop in school performance

- loss of interest or pleasure in activities once enjoyed

- outbursts of shouting, complaining, unexplained irritability or crying

- thoughts of death or suicide

- expressions of fear or anxiety

- aggression, refusal to cooperate or antisocial behavior

- use of alcohol or other drugs

- constant complaints of aching arms, legs, or stomach with no apparent cause

The APA advocates treating children struggling with depression as essential; it frees them to develop necessary academic and social skills. During psychotherapy, children learn to express their feelings and to develop ways of coping with their illness. Some children also respond to antidepressant medications whose use must be closely monitored. Psychiatric medication shouldn't be the only form of treatment, but rather should be part of a comprehensive program.

Attention-Deficit/Hyperactivity Disorder

If you have a child who has been diagnosed with Attention-Deficit/ Hyperactivity Disorder participating in your program, there may be specific requirements or medications involved in his or her care. The main features of ADHD include hyperactivity, impulsiveness, and an inability to sustain attention or concentration. These main symptoms occur at levels that cause significant distress and impairment and are far more severe than typically found in children of similar age and developmental level. ADHD is found in 3 percent to 5 percent of all school-age children. Much more common in boys than in girls, this disorder often develops before age 7 but is most often diagnosed when the child is between ages 8 and 10. Children with ADHD

- have difficulty finishing any activity that requires concentration.

- don't seem to listen to anything said to them.

- are excessively active — running or climbing at inappropriate times, squirming in or jumping out of their seats.

- are very easily distracted.

- talk incessantly, often blurting out responses before questions are finished.

- have serious difficulty waiting their turn in games or groups.

In addition, children with ADHD may have specific learning disabilities, which can lead to emotional problems as a result of falling behind in school or receiving constant reprimands from adults or ridicule from other children.

Suicidal Clues

- ❏ change in eating and sleeping habits
- ❏ drug and alcohol abuse
- ❏ noticeable personality change
- ❏ violent reactions, rebellious behavior, running away
- ❏ persistent boredom, difficulty concentrating, falling grades
- ❏ loss of interest in fun activities
- ❏ focus on morbid or death themes
- ❏ frequent complaints of stomachaches, headaches, and fatigue — physical symptoms often related to emotions
- ❏ intolerance for praise or rewards
- ❏ prior attempt at suicide
- ❏ family history of suicide
- ❏ complaints of feeling "rotten inside"
- ❏ verbal hints such as "I won't be a problem to you much longer; nothing matters; it's no use; I won't see you again; I wish I was never born"
- ❏ putting affairs in order, cleaning room, throwing or giving away important belongings
- ❏ suddenly becoming cheerful after a period of depression

Adapted from an American Academy of Pediatrics fact sheet.

Treatment can include the use of medications, special educational programs to help the child keep up academically, and psychotherapy. Between 70 and 80 percent of children with ADHD respond to medications, which allow them a chance to improve their attention span, perform tasks better and control impulsive behavior. As a result, children get along better with their teachers, classmates and parents, which, in turn, improves their self-esteem. Psychotherapy enables children to cope with their disorder and the reaction of others to it. An essential component of psychotherapy involves the child psychiatrist working with both the child and the parents to develop techniques for behavior management.

Suicide

According to the Centers for Disease Control, suicide is the third leading cause of death for 15 to 24 year olds, and the sixth leading cause of death for 5 to 14 year olds. Often youths considering suicide exhibit behavioral clues, which your staff members should be able to recognize.

The strongest risk factors for attempted suicide in youth are depression, alcohol or drug abuse, aggressive or disruptive behaviors, and sexual orientation.

Adolescents who consider suicide generally feel alone, hopeless and rejected. They are especially vulnerable to these feelings if they have experienced a loss, humiliation or trauma. These might be poor performance on a test; breakup with a boyfriend or girlfriend; parents with alcohol or drug problems or who are abusive; or a family life affected by parental discord, separation, or divorce. However, a teenager still may be depressed or suicidal even without any of these adverse conditions.

Teenagers who are planning to commit suicide might "clean house" by giving away favorite possessions, cleaning their rooms or throwing things away. After a period of depression, they may also become suddenly cheerful because they think that by deciding to end their lives they have "found the solution." According to the American Academy of Child and Adolescent Psychiatry, young people who have attempted suicide in the past or who talk about suicide are at greater risk for future attempts. Listen for hints like "I'd be better off dead" or "I won't be a problem for you much longer."

What Can Be Done?

Teens aren't helped by lectures or by hearing all the reasons they have to live. What they need is to be reassured that they have someone to whom they can turn — be it family, friends, school counselor, physician or teacher — to discuss their feelings or problems. It must be a person who is very willing to listen and who is able to reassure the individual that depression and suicidal tendencies can be treated. This means that the organization should consider training the staff members who interact with participants to recognize statements or actions that are cries for help from a teen considering suicide.

Staff members should take these cries for help seriously and respond in a caring, and not a derogatory way, to the teen. Threats of suicide, or other signs that a child is contemplating suicide should be reported to a specified staff member who is responsible for assessing the situation and taking action such as offering counseling, making a referral, and discussing their concerns with the child's parents.

Unless the organization includes suicide interventions in its mission and has staff qualified to offer the necessary services, informing the parents and encouraging a follow-up with a qualified mental health professional is extremely important. Local chapters of the American Psychiatric Association can help by recommending a psychiatrist, a physician with special training in emotional and mental health. Help can also be found through local mental health associations, family physicians, a county medical society, a local hospital's department of psychiatry, a community mental health center, a mood disorders program affiliated with a university or medical school, or a family service/social service agency.

In short, simply taking the time to talk to troubled teenagers about their emotions or problems can help prevent the senseless tragedy of teen suicide. Let them know help is available and encourage them to seek it. Do not promise to keep their suicidal ideation or acts secret. The organization must notify the child's parents.

Drug and Alcohol Abuse

Drug and alcohol abuse may be found in all socioeconomic levels and in all racial and ethnic groups. While drug and alcohol abuse most often affects adolescents, it isn't uncommon to discover younger children experimenting with various illegal substances.

A yearly survey of students in 8th through 12th grade shows that 23 percent of 8th graders have tried marijuana at least once, and by 10th grade, 21 percent are "current" users (that is, used within the past month). Among 12th graders, nearly 50 percent have tried marijuana/hash at least once, and about 24 percent were current users.

Alcohol Abuse

Monitoring the Future, an annual survey of alcohol and drug use by U.S. students, has shown consistently that alcohol is the drug most often used and abused by children and adolescents. The study of U.S. students in the 8th, 10th and 12th grades, which was conducted in 2000 by the University of Michigan Institute for Social Research, shows alcohol use by teens has remained fairly stable in recent years. Nearly a quarter (22 percent) of the 8th graders report having taken an alcoholic beverage in the last 30 days, and exactly half (50 percent) of the 12th graders report having done so. One in every 12 (8.3 percent) 8th graders reports being drunk at least once in the past 30 days, as do a third (32.3 percent) of the 12th graders. "These rates are high by most people's standards," comments researcher Lloyd D. Johnston, "but about where they have been over the past several years." *Monitoring the Future* has been conducted annually starting in 1991.

Alcohol use frequently occurs before or during early adolescence. A retrospective report among students who have used alcohol indicated that 11 percent had their first drink by 6th grade, 38 percent by 8th grade, and 60 percent by 9th grade. Between 4 percent and 9 percent of 8th, 10th, and 12th graders admit to having been drunk by the 6th grade.

The American Academy of Pediatrics states that alcohol is often called a "gateway drug." When young people like the feeling they get from alcohol,

Alcohol-related Risks

Alcohol is linked with a variety of risky behaviors, and outcomes such as:

❑ *Crime and serious violence.*

❑ *Early sexual activity, multiple partners, sexually transmitted diseases including AIDS, and unintended teenage pregnancy.*

❑ *Fetal Alcohol Syndrome.* Drinking during pregnancy can cause a baby to be born with major birth defects. No one knows exactly how much alcohol is too much during pregnancy, but it's known that the more a mother drinks, the greater the risk to her baby.

❑ *Drunk driving.* It's the leading cause of death for young adults, aged 15 to 24 years. In one study, an estimated 6 to 14 percent of drivers younger than 21 years who were stopped at roadside checkpoints had been drinking. This age group makes up only 20 percent of the licensed drivers in the United States, yet these drivers are involved in almost 50 percent of all fatal car crashes.

they may be interested in trying other drugs later. This can lead to multiple drug use, which is very dangerous. The use of alcohol by itself or with other drugs can harm a child's normal growth and development.

Even if a teenager only drinks occasionally, intoxicated behavior can be lethal. Just one drink can impair decision-making and slow down reaction time in any situation.

Most adolescents never move beyond the first stage of alcohol use. Whether they do or not depends for the most part on their personality, their family and their community. For those who move to the advanced stages, the entire process can take months or years. Early detection is important. Many young people and adults receive help too late.

With a current emphasis on the dangers of underage drinking, you may wonder why young people continue to drink alcohol. There are a variety of reasons indicated by the American Academy of Pediatrics:

- Curiosity. They have heard that getting drunk is fun and they want to find out for themselves.

- They see drinking as a "rite of passage" — something to be experienced on the way to adulthood.

- To get drunk. This explains why they often drink until they are out of control. Binge drinking (consuming five or more drinks in a row for males, four for females) is alarmingly common. Sixteen percent of 8th graders, 25 percent of 10th graders, and 30 percent of high school seniors have reported binge drinking.

- To fit in with friends who are already using alcohol.

- To feel relaxed and to boost self-confidence.

- To escape problems, such as depression, family conflict, trouble in school or with a boyfriend or girlfriend.

Marijuana

The National Institute on Drug Abuse states that marijuana is a green, brown or gray mixture of dried, shredded leaves, stems, seeds and flowers of the hemp plant *(Cannabis sativa)*. Cannabis is a term that refers to marijuana and other drugs made from the same plant. Strong forms of cannabis include sinse-milla (sin-seh-me-yah), hashish ("hash" for short) and hash oil. All forms of cannabis are mind-altering (psychoactive) drugs; they all contain THC (delta-9-tetrahydrocannabinol), the main active chemical in marijuana. They also contain more than 400 other chemicals.

Marijuana's effect on the user depends on the strength or potency of the THC it contains. THC potency had increased in the 1970s but has been about the same since the mid-1980s. The strength of the drug is measured by the average amount of THC in test samples confiscated by law enforcement agencies.

A University of Michigan yearly survey of students in grades 8 through 12 shows that 23 percent of 8th graders have tried marijuana at least once, and by 10th grade, 21 percent are "current" users (that is, used within the past month). Among 12th graders, nearly 50 percent have tried marijuana/hash at least once, and about 24 percent were current users. Other researchers have found that use of marijuana and other drugs usually peaks in the late teens and early 20s, then declines in later years.

If someone is high on marijuana, he or she might:

- seem dizzy and have trouble walking;
- seem silly and giggly for no reason;
- have very red, bloodshot eyes; and
- have a hard time remembering things that just happened.

When the early effects fade, over a few hours, the user can become very sleepy.

Inhalants

The National Institutes of Health points out that most inhalants are common household products that give off mind-altering chemical fumes when sniffed. These common products include paint thinner, fingernail polish remover, glues, gasoline, cigarette lighter fluid and nitrous oxide. They also include fluorinated hydrocarbons found in aerosols, such as whipped cream, hair and paint sprays, and computer cleaners.

If someone is an inhalant abuser, the National Inhalant Abuse Prevention Center says some or all these symptoms may be evident:

- unusual breath odor or chemical odor on clothing.
- slurred or disoriented speech.
- drunk, dazed or dizzy appearance.
- signs of paint or other products where they wouldn't normally be, such as on the face or fingers.
- red or runny eyes or nose.
- spots and/or sores around the mouth.
- nausea and/or loss of appetite.
- chronic inhalant abusers may exhibit such symptoms as anxiety, excitability, irritability or restlessness.

Anabolic Steroids

The National Institute on Drug Abuse (NIDA), in its nationwide 1999 *Monitoring the Future* survey of drug abuse among adolescents in middle and high schools, estimated that 2.7 percent of 8th and 10th graders and 2.9 percent of 12th graders had taken anabolic steroids at least once in their lives. For 10th graders, that is a significant increase from 1998, when 2.0 percent of 10th graders said they had taken anabolic steroids at least once. For all three grades, the 1999 levels represent a significant increase from 1991, the first year that data on steroid abuse were collected from the younger students. In that year, 1.9 percent of 8th graders, 1.8 percent of 10th graders, and 2.1 percent of 12th graders reported that they had taken anabolic steroids at least once.

Anabolic steroids are chemicals that are similar to the male sex hormone testosterone and are used by an increasing number of young people to enhance their muscle size. While anabolic steroids are quite successful at building muscle, they can damage many body organs, including the liver, kidneys and heart. They may also trigger dependency in users, particularly when taken in the large doses that have been known to be used by many bodybuilders and athletes, reports the National Clearinghouse for Alcohol and Drug Information.

The physical and psychological risks of anabolic steroid use include:

- damage to growth areas at the end of bones, permanently stunting growth;

- weakened tendons, resulting in tearing or rupture;

- facial hair, lower voice, and irregular menstrual periods for young women;

- acne, loss of hair, and testicular shrinkage for young men;

- infection with HIV through sharing needles to inject steroids; and

- depression, aggressiveness or combativeness.

Club Drugs

According to NIDA, "club drug" is a vague term that refers to a wide variety of drugs. These drugs include *MDMA* (Ecstasy), *GHB, Rohypnol, ketamine, methamphetamine,* and *LSD,* all of which are gaining popularity. Uncertainties about the drug sources, pharmacological agents, chemicals used to manufacture them and possible contaminants make it difficult to determine toxicity, consequences and symptoms that might be expected in a particular community.

No club drug is benign. Chronic abuse of MDMA, for example, appears to produce long-term damage to serotonin-containing neurons in the brain. Given the important role that the neurotransmitter serotonin plays in regulating emotion, memory, sleep, pain and higher-order cognitive processes, it's likely that MDMA use can cause a variety of behavioral and cognitive consequences, as well as impairing memory.

Because some club drugs are colorless, tasteless and odorless, they can be added unobtrusively to beverages by individuals who want to intoxicate or sedate others. In recent years, reports of club drugs being used to commit sexual assaults have increased — yet another reason why NIDA finds these escalating trends disturbing.

Responding to the Challenge of Alcohol and Drug Abuse

The National Institutes of Health offers the following suggestions.

Prevention programs should:

❑ be designed to enhance "protective factors" and move toward reversing or reducing known "risk factors."

❑ target all forms of drug abuse, including the use of tobacco, alcohol, marijuana, and inhalants.

❑ include skills to resist drugs when offered, strengthen personal commitments against drug use, and increase social competency, in conjunction with reinforcement of attitudes against drug use.

❑ include interactive methods, such as peer discussion groups, rather than didactic teaching techniques alone when targeting adolescents.

❑ include a parents' or caregivers' component that reinforces what the children are learning and that opens opportunities for family discussions about use of legal and illegal substances and family policies about their use.

❑ be long-term, over the school career with repeat interventions to reinforce the original prevention goals. For example, school-based efforts directed at elementary and middle school students should include booster sessions to help with critical transitions from middle to high school.

❑ be adapted to address the specific nature of the drug abuse problem in the local community.

❑ be age-specific, developmentally appropriate, and culturally sensitive.

❑ be cost-effective. For every dollar spent on drug use prevention, communities can save $4 to $5 in costs for drug abuse treatment and counseling.

❑ proportionate to the level of risk in the target population. The higher the level of risk, the more intensive the prevention effort must be and the earlier it must begin.

❑ be family-focused. These have a greater impact than strategies that focus on parents only or children only.

Community programs:

❑ that include media campaigns and policy changes, such as new regulations that restrict access to alcohol, tobacco, or other drugs, are more effective when school and family interventions accompany them.

❑ need to strengthen norms against drug use in all drug abuse prevention settings, including the family, the school, and the community.

School programs:

❑ offer opportunities to reach all populations and also serve as important settings for specific sub-populations at risk for drug abuse, such as children with behavior problems or learning disabilities and those who are potential dropouts.

Source: National Institute on Drug Abuse, National Institutes of Health. For copies of the booklet Preventing Drug Use Among Children and Adolescents, *call the National Clearinghouse for Alcohol and Drug Information at (800) 729-6686.*

Managing Health Related Risks

The keys to managing health-related risks in youth-serving organizations are very similar to managing other kinds of risks. Effective risk reduction strategies rely upon a combination of personnel, program, premises and participant-related measures.

Personnel

Intelligent observation is a key requirement for staff members of youth-serving programs. Staff members need to be trained to look for health-related risks and risk-oriented behavior in the young people participating in the organization's program. For example, when a tot arrives in the morning at the childcare center, the staff members need to be aware of the physical condition of the child. Does the child appear to be healthy? Are there any visible cuts or bruises? Does the child appear to move in a normal fashion? Are there any signs of illness — fever, redness of eyes or runny nose? Does the child meet an acceptable level of personal hygiene? Observations should be recorded along with any remedial actions the organization takes.

In programs for older children, staff should be alert to any signs of depression, behaviors that might indicate drug or alcohol abuse and failure to comply with safety rules for the specific activity.

As role models, staff members should avoid glamorizing or making light of drug or alcohol involvement by the young people in the program. From a safety perspective, nonprofits should establish a zero-tolerance policy for staff members who show up to work with children and are under the influence of alcohol or illegal drugs.

Program

When a child participates in a program in which the organization assumes responsibility for the supervision and care of the child, the program should insist on completion of a health history and medical release by the parents. This should alert the staff of the program to any existing health problems — including allergies and medications — and permit the organization to obtain medical assistance when necessary.

When a child has a health condition noted on the medical history form, all staff members need to be alerted about the condition and its implications for the child's participation in the program. For example, if the child has an allergy to peanuts noted on the health form, it's not a good idea to include the child in a cooking class in which baking peanut butter cookies will be the day's activity. In fact, any sensitivity to peanuts may be grounds to avoid peanut products throughout the program. Baking sugar cookies would be a more appropriate activity selection.

Some children will have health problems that require them to restrict their activities, take medications, or may require other kinds of specific care. To the extent that programs can reasonably accommodate these needs, they may be required to do so under Title II of the Americans with Disabilities Act. Even without a legal requirement, making provision for children with special needs in most nonprofits' programs is in keeping with their mission statements.

Premises

Whether it's ensuring access to children with disabilities or taking steps to prevent children with contagious diseases from infecting others within the program, the physical environment influences the health and safety of the children being served there.

Interior Air Quality

According to the Environmental Protection Agency, the term "sick building syndrome" is used to describe situations in which building occupants experience acute health and comfort effects that appear to be linked to time spent in a building, but no specific illness or cause can be identified. The complaints may be localized in a particular room or zone, or may be widespread throughout the building. In contrast, the term "building related illness" is used when symptoms of diagnosable illness are identified and can be attributed directly to airborne building contaminants. While more commonly related to employee- related issues, the conditions that cause SBS and BRI may also contribute to the health problems of children or exacerbate existing allergies.

The following have been cited causes of or contributing factors to sick building syndrome:

❑ inadequate ventilation;

❑ chemical contaminants from indoor sources such as carpets, adhesives, detergents, solvents and chemicals used in office machines;

❑ chemical contaminants from outdoor sources — such as pollutants from motor vehicle exhausts — plumbing vents and building exhausts — bathrooms and kitchens — can enter the building through poorly located air intake vents, windows, and other openings; and

❑ biological contaminants, such as bacteria, molds, pollen and viruses, may breed in stagnant water that has accumulated in ducts, humidifiers and drain pans, or where water has collected on ceiling tiles, carpeting or insulation. Sometimes insects or bird droppings can be a source of biological contaminants.

The National Educational Association points to a number of conditions in school buildings that contribute to health problems in children. These include the age of the buildings, lack of money for renovations and repairs, and overcrowding. All of these factors may also be found in many facilities used by nonprofit organizations for serving children.

Cleanliness

The National Network for Child Care suggests that careful, routine cleaning of surfaces and toys also greatly reduces the spread of germs. There are many excellent cleansers and disinfectants available for commercial use. Scrubbing surfaces and toys with soap and water is a good way to start, but in places where group activities take place, regular use of a disinfectant or a disinfectant cleanser is safer.

Toxic substances

Asbestos and lead are two toxic substances that are often found in older buildings. Radon gas is another toxic material that infiltrates buildings and may cause long-term health problems for those who are exposed to it. In the past several years, public awareness of the harmful effects of these substances has increased and the Environmental Protection Agency and many state and local health departments have published regulations concerning abatement and removal of each of these. When concerning the use of a facility for programs for children, organizations should inspect the facilities to ensure that toxic substances aren't present in forms that could harm the health of the children participating in the program.

Participants

Organizations have the responsibility to take reasonable measures to protect the health and safety of the participants in their programs. In some cases, for example summer camps and other residential programs, participants may require medication that must be administered by the staff. This is a serious responsibility and one in which adherence to policies is mandatory.

Dispensing Medication

The following guidelines are suggested for dispensing medication to children in your program:

- ❑ Have the child's parent or legal guardian complete and sign a Medication Release Form for each medication.

- ❑ Give only medicine (prescription or over-the-counter) that is in the original container. It should be labeled with the child's name, correct dosage, and the name of the pharmacy that supplied the medicine. If you have any questions, contact the child's medical professional or pharmacist.

- ❑ Don't give any child medication that was prescribed for another child even if it appears to be the same medication. If a child needs additional medication, contact the child's parents, the child's physician or pharmacist. If an emergency situation arises due to missed medication, contact the nearest emergency room.

- ❑ You need *parental permission* to administer the following non-prescription medications (*medical permission* is *not* required):

  - antihistamines
  - non-aspirin pain relievers and fever reducers
  - cough medicine
  - decongestants
  - anti-itching creams
  - diaper ointments and powders
  - sunscreen

- ❑ Use an accurate medicine dropper or measuring spoon. Regular silverware spoons are *not* acceptable for measuring medicine.

- ❑ Stop giving medication if you observe side effects. Inform parents and/or medical professional.

- ❑ Keep a small notebook and record of each dosage of medicine that you give any child. Note child's name, medication, dose, date and time of day.

When a participant in your program self-medicates (for example, a child with asthma uses an inhaler on an as-needed basis), consult with the child's parents and child's physician to determine the degree to which the organization needs to supervise the child's usage. Document the agreement with a contract between the participant, parent, program staff and child's physician. The following is an example of a contract suggested for schools by the National Heart, Lung and Blood Institute in their publication, *Managing Asthma: A Guide for Schools*, NIH Publication 91-2650.

If your organization allows participants to administer their own medications, it's important to stress with the participants that they should *never* share their medications with other participants. There is a risk that young people will feel less cautious about sharing their medications and for that reason, organizations may decide to store all medications in a central location where dispensing them can be supervised by a staff member.

Over the Counter Drugs

Youth-serving organization should establish a policy for possession of over the counter medications by participants. The policy should consider the age of the participants and the nature of the medications to be encompassed by the policy. According to media reports, some schools have implemented policies under the auspices of their "zero tolerance" for drugs that would prohibit students from possessing over the counter antacids. It's important to be mindful that many OTC medications have serious side effects when misused and should be controlled when used by participants, for example many cough suppressants have high levels of alcohol and may be used by students to become inebriated.

S A M P L E
Permission Slip
For permission to carry inhalers

1. Student has demonstrated to the nurse correct use of inhaler.
2. Student agrees to never share the inhaler with another person.
3. Student agrees that after two puffs, if there isn't marked improvement, he/she will go to see the nurse immediately.

Student's signature_____

I give permission for my child_____
to carry the inhaler described below. I understand that he/she must follow the rules listed above. I will notify the school of changes in medication or my child's condition.

Name of Medication   Dose   Frequency of Use

_____   _____   _____

_____   _____   _____

Parent's signature: _____

Date: _____

Appropriate referrals

Nonprofits must recognize their own limitations in dealing with some kinds of health problems that children may present. For example, a staff member may recognize the signs of depression being exhibited by a child in the program and attempt to counsel the child beyond the staff member's qualifications. A more appropriate course of action would be to offer emotional support for the child, but to refer the child and the child's parents to a qualified mental health professional or mental health center for assistance. The child will be more assured of getting the needed treatment and the nonprofit will avoid the tragedy of bearing some of the responsibility if the child becomes suicidal.

Epilogue

Youth would be an ideal state if it came a little later in life.

— Herbert Asquith

The wealth of experiences provided to young people through youth-servingnonprofits equips tomorrow's adults with social and vocational skills. During this season of hope, your nonprofit's risk management strategies can nurture children in your programs while they explore, stretch and grow. By providing age-appropriate toys, games and equipment; educating supervisors for their roles; sharing behavioral expectations and following through on consequences if behaviors aren't appropriate; and keeping your premises and equipment well maintained and in good repair your nonprofit will be well on its way to balancing risk and reward.

Look on risk management as a tool to protect children. This isn't a cookie cutter approach. Because each youth-serving organization, although somewhat alike, has its own program and activities related to its mission each organization has to develop its own risk management recipes. This will enable the children and your nonprofit to prosper and grow.

As you develop your risk management plan, you'll find that risk management strategies presented in the previous chapters relate to more than one issue. For instance, as you're screening potential staff members, think about all the exposures your organizations has that could be reduced by asking the right questions or looking for the right "red flags." The question you should be addressing is "What kind of screening process should your organization develop to ensure that you have the right staff?" The answer is "One that can deliver your program safely." Planning ahead can help you identify the people with the appropriate skills and characteristics for working with your young participants. As you review your policies and procedures, what updating, additions or deletions need to be made considering all of the risks to which your service recipients and your organization may be exposed? This isn't an all-inclusive summary.

The matrix on the next page lists risk exposures and risk management strategies as identified in this book. You should decide which are applicable to your nonprofit and the risks you face. Some of the risk control strategies may not apply to your specific risks, in which case, you need to satisfy yourself that each risk you have identified for your organization has been examined and reasonable steps are being taken to address that risk. *The Season of Hope* is designed to help program managers, agency and organization executives, board members and paid and volunteer staff to be more alert to potential dangers and determine what they can do about them. If you do this, we think you'll have a good start on developing sound risk management strategies.

If after reading this book, you have further questions or wish additional assistance in developing risk management strategies for your youth-serving programs, please visit our Web site at www.nonprofitrisk.org, or call the Nonprofit Risk Management Center at (202) 785-3891. The Center's staff can assist you in many ways in the short term or long term. They can answer technical questions, refer you to additional publications, tell you about a self-assessment CD-ROM, provide a risk assessment or work with you to build creative solutions specific to your nonprofit's needs. From publications to consulting services, the Nonprofit Risk Management Center is here to help.

Relationship Between Risk Exposures and Risk Modification Strategies

Youth-serving organizations find risk management is the most successful when they evaluate the whole child in the context of the whole program. The matrix at right will provide a structure for you to do just that.

While it's important to look at how each of the risk control strategies (the horizontal row) can impact each exposure, it's just as important to look down the risk exposures (the vertical column) to see how each risk control strategy may relate to each exposure. For example, as you develop your staff training, have you considered how it can be used to improve parental relationships and communication thereby lowering some risks? What other exposures should your organization's training program address that would improve the safety of its children?

Relationship of Risk Exposures to Risk Control Strategies

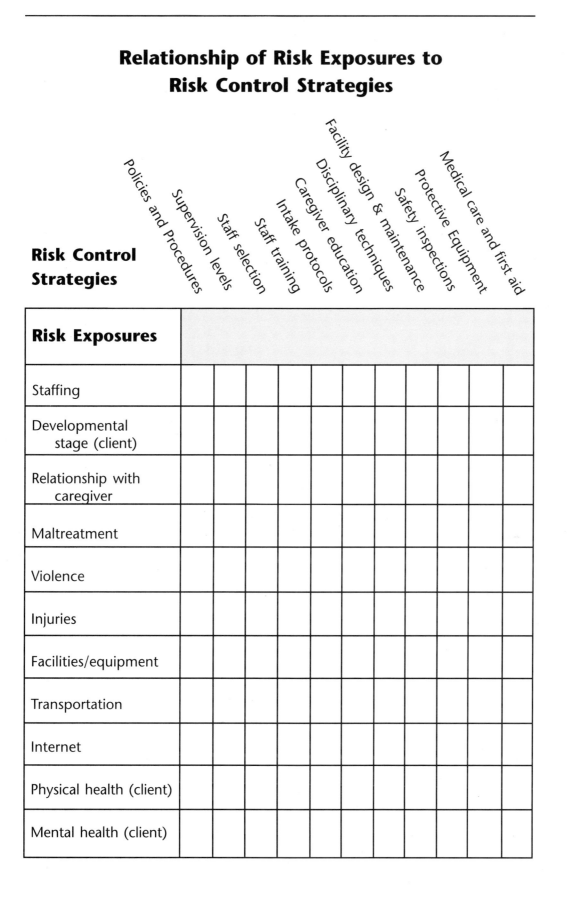

Risk Control Strategies / Risk Exposures	Policies and Procedures	Supervision levels	Staff selection	Staff training	Intake protocols	Caregiver education	Disciplinary techniques	Facility design & maintenance	Safety inspections	Protective Equipment	Medical care and first aid
Staffing											
Developmental stage (client)											
Relationship with caregiver											
Maltreatment											
Violence											
Injuries											
Facilities/equipment											
Transportation											
Internet											
Physical health (client)											
Mental health (client)											

Checklists

Checklist for Risk Management Strategies in Youth-Serving Nonprofits

Personnel

- ❑ Written position descriptions for both employees and volunteers.
- ❑ Basic application process for every position that includes:
  - ❑ Written application.
  - ❑ Face-to-face interviews.
  - ❑ At least three personal or professional references checked.
- ❑ For positions that entail more extensive, unsupervised contact with children:
  - ❑ Criminal history record checks (state level).
  - ❑ Additional reference checking.
  - ❑ Sex offender registry record check.
  - ❑ Fingerprint-based FBI national record checks for individuals who have not resided in the state for five years.
  - ❑ Compliance with state laws regarding screening of personnel (if applicable).
- ❑ For positions that involve operating motor vehicles and transporting children:
  - ❑ Department of Motor Vehicles record checks.

- ❑ Verification of credentials (if related to position responsibilities).

- ❑ Orientation program for new staff members (both volunteers and employees) to acquaint them with the organization's policies and procedures regarding:
  - ❑ Organization's mission.
  - ❑ Discipline.
  - ❑ Reporting suspected child abuse.
  - ❑ Responding to emergencies.
  - ❑ Maintaining sufficient adult presence to avoid one-on-one contact between child and adult.
  - ❑ Confidentiality of clientele information.
  - ❑ Intervention in child-to-child violence.
  - ❑ Incident reporting requirements.
  - ❑ Toileting, showering, and other situations in which children are changing clothes or bathing.
  - ❑ Sexual harassment policy.
  - ❑ Media contacts.
- ❑ In-service training for all staff members to recognize signs of problems and respond appropriately:
  - ❑ Depression
  - ❑ Suicidal tendencies
  - ❑ Child abuse and neglect
  - ❑ Gang activity

- ❑ Violence/weapons
- ❑ Drug and alcohol abuse
- ❑ Children with disabilities
- ❑ Supervisors receive training specific to their supervisory responsibilities.

Program

- ❑ Activities have adequate supervision to ensure safety of participants.
- ❑ Activities are age appropriate.
- ❑ Equipment used in program activities meets safety standards for the activity.
- ❑ Parental involvement is welcomed.
- ❑ Use of appropriate protective equipment is required for activities.
- ❑ First aid and emergency medical care have been prearranged.
- ❑ Proper preparation is required for activities that require physical stamina and skills.
- ❑ Physical activities are curtailed when weather is too hot or cold to conduct activity safely.
- ❑ Drinking water is available and youngsters are encouraged to drink to avoid dehydration when participating in activities requiring physical exertion causing them to perspire.

Premises

- ❑ First aid and emergency medical care have been prearranged.
- ❑ Regular safety inspections conducted.
- ❑ Procedures for reporting and repairing unsafe conditions.
- ❑ Smoke detectors, fire extinguishers and sprinkler systems operable.
- ❑ Flammable materials stored in metal, fire resistant locker.
- ❑ Staff members are familiar with location of electrical circuit breakers and fuse boxes.
- ❑ Meets or exceeds licensing standards (if applicable).
- ❑ Exits are clearly marked and able to be opened from the inside in case of emergency.
- ❑ Access to premises can be controlled and monitored.
- ❑ Premises free of toxic materials such as lead-based paints and asbestos.
- ❑ Outdoor venues checked for hazardous conditions and poisonous plants.
- ❑ Hazardous areas marked with appropriate warnings or fenced.

Safety Checklist for Child-care Providers

Parking lot

- ❑ The surface is clear of ice and snow.
- ❑ The lot is designed so pedestrians don't need to walk between cars.
- ❑ Cars aren't left running while unattended.
- ❑ Children are supervised by an adult and not allowed to run into the lot.

Entrance

- ❑ All stairs have handrails.
- ❑ Entrance and exit are at sidewalk level or onto same-level landing.

❏ All elevated areas (porches, landings) are fenced with vertical pickets less than four inches apart.

❏ Doors open outward and are never locked from the inside.

❏ Monitoring is done to prevent strangers from entering the facility.

Hallways and Stairways

❏ Areas are kept clean and unobstructed (prevent injury and fire hazard).

❏ Lighting is adequate.

❏ Exits are well-marked, lighted and unobstructed.

❏ All sharp edges on corners or counters are covered.

❏ Safety glass is used in doors and windows.

❏ Stairways are carpeted and have a child-height railing on the right side for descending.

❏ Smoke detectors are working.

❏ There is no visible peeling paint; lead-based paint isn't used.

Rooms and Storage Units

❏ Electrical sockets are high and out of reach or securely covered.

❏ No electrical cords are dangling or covered.

❏ Cabinets or file boxes that contain medications and diluted cleaning solutions are locked.

❏ Concentrated solutions aren't kept in the classroom or playroom.

❏ All hardware on cribs, tables and bookcases is checked monthly to make certain screws and bolts are tight.

❏ Hot plates aren't used.

❏ Chairs or tables aren't used as ladders to hang items.

❏ No sharp corners are exposed on tables or other furniture.

❏ Toys are safe: no sharp areas, pinch points or small parts.

❏ Fire exit from room requires only one turn or pull-down action to open door.

❏ Accessible above-ground-level windows are protected with grills or screens.

❏ Hot surfaces, hot pipes, heaters and vents are out of reach of children; space heaters aren't used.

❏ Temperature of tap water for hand washing is 120° F. or less.

❏ Lighting is adequate in all rooms.

❏ Walkways between sleeping cots are clear for children and staff.

❏ Children are supervised in high chairs and chairs.

❏ Infant walkers aren't used.

❏ Pacifiers must have strings less than six inches long.

❏ Emergency phone is accessible.

❏ Trashcans are covered and secured.

❏ No smoking is allowed.

❏ Floors are smooth, clean and not slippery.

Kitchen

❏ Only authorized personnel are allowed in the kitchen.

❏ Sharp utensils are kept out of reach of children.

❏ All containers are clearly marked and have secure lids.

❏ Fire extinguishers are easily accessible.

- ❑ Items on shelving units are neatly organized, secure and not piled high.
- ❑ Separate sinks are used for hand washing and food preparation.

Bathrooms

- ❑ Cleaning supplies aren't accessible.
- ❑ Toilets and sinks are appropriate for use by children; step stools are provided.
- ❑ Water temperature for hand washing is maintained at 120° F or less.
- ❑ Floors are nonskid.

Outdoor Playground

- ❑ Equipment is checked weekly for sharp protrusions.
- ❑ Bolts are covered; swings have soft seats.
- ❑ Ground is covered with loose-fill surface material.
- ❑ Play area is fenced; gate has safety locks.
- ❑ Equipment is age-appropriate; slides are enclosed or have handrails; only one child at a time uses the equipment; and there are no spaces 3.5 to 9 inches where a child's head, leg or arm could be trapped.
- ❑ Constant supervision is provided.
- ❑ No poisonous plants, trash or sharp objects are in the area surrounding the playground.

Toxic Chemicals

- ❑ Kitchen and cleaning supplies have their own locked storage unit.
- ❑ Cleaning solutions for use in classrooms and playrooms are stored in a locked closet.

Computers, TVs and Electrical Equipment

- ❑ The equipment is flush against the wall covering the electrical outlet.
- ❑ Only authorized people service the equipment.
- ❑ Liquids aren't allowed near equipment.
- ❑ Children are supervised while equipment is in use.

Vans and Other Vehicles

- ❑ First aid kit is available.
- ❑ Child-restraint devices are appropriate for child's size and weight.
- ❑ Seat belts are used and maintained.
- ❑ Radio sound level is kept at a minimum and the program content is appropriate for children.
- ❑ Vehicle tires, oil and brakes are maintained regularly.
- ❑ Driver has a current license that authorizes operation of the vehicle driven and is trained to operate said vehicle.
- ❑ Children aren't allowed in the front seat.
- ❑ Vehicle is checked for sharp or rusty metal.

Staff Training

- ❑ A person who is certified in pediatric first aid, including rescue breathing and first aid for choking is on the premises at all times.
- ❑ Children are taught safety and emergency procedures.
- ❑ Staff is fully trained in emergency procedures.

Art Supplies

❑ Nontoxic art supplies, such as natural dyes and water-based products are used.

❑ Scissors use is supervised.

❑ Aerosol sprays and solvent-based glues are avoided.

Field Trips

❑ Child-care center or camp personnel provide adequate supervision.

❑ Each child wears identification.

❑ Young children hold hands in pairs or hold onto a rope when walking in a group.

Equipment

❑ First aid kit is appropriately stocked.

❑ Sports equipment is safe and soft.

Fire and Severe Weather Drills

❑ All children are safely evacuated to a safe area within three minutes.

❑ Monthly fire drills are held.

❑ Smoke detectors and the alarm system are in place and working.

Adapted from Injury Prevention and Control for Children and Youth *by the American Academy of Pediatrics.*

Child-care Facility Safety Checklist

❑ Children greeted when arrive and acknowledged when they depart?
❑ Caregivers trained in pediatric first aid?
❑ Injuries are recorded in logbook?
❑ Emergency phone numbers posted by telephone?
❑ Plastic bags are stored out of sight and out of reach?
❑ Playground equipment is secured on an energy-absorbing surface?
❑ List of children and their allergies in classroom and kitchen?
❑ Hot water temperature at the tap is 120°F or less?
❑ Barriers on stairs are adequate to prevent children from falling?
❑ Screens cover all heat sources?
❑ Smoke detectors are in each area of the center?
❑ Smoke detectors are checked monthly?
❑ High chairs have safety harnesses?
❑ Cribs are sturdy with hardware in good condition?
❑ Changing tables have sides to prevent infants from rolling off?
❑ Outdoor play areas are adequately fenced?
❑ The caregiver can see the entire playground?
❑ The playground is free of hazardous litter (rocks, cans and bottles)?
❑ Children in the after-school program use the playground at a different time than younger children?
❑ Sandboxes are covered?
❑ Sports equipment is soft?

Adapted from page 80 in *Injury Prevention and Control for Children and Youth* published by the American Academy of Pediatrics.

Resources

Access Board, The
1331 F St., NW, Suite 1000
Washington, DC 20004-1111
Tel: (202) 272-5434; (800) 872-2253
TTY: (202) 272-5449 ; (800) 993-2822
Fax: (202) 272-5447
e-mail: info@access-board.gov
www.access-board.gov

A Guideline for ADA Accessible Guidelines to Play Areas (pdf), published by U.S.
Architectural Barriers Compliance Board, May 2001.
www.access-board.gov/play/guide/intro.htm

American Academy of Child and Adolescent Psychiatry
3615 Wisconsin Ave., N.W.
Washington, DC 20016-3007
Tel: (202) 966-7300
Fax: (202) 966-2891
www.aacap.org

AACAP, a 501(c)(3) non-profit organization established in 1953, is the leading national
professional medical association dedicated to treating and improving the quality of life
for children, adolescents and families affected by mental, behavioral or developmental
disorders. The academy's Web site offers information on child and adolescent
psychiatry, and fact sheets for parents and caregivers.

American Academy of Pediatrics
141 Northwest Point Blvd.
Elk Grove Village, IL 60007- 1098
Tel: (847) 434-4000
Fax: (847) 434-8000
www.aap.org

AAP, founded in 1930, dedicates its efforts and resources to the health, safety and well-being of infants, children, adolescents and young adults. The AAP has approximately 55,000 member pediatricians, pediatric medical subspecialists and pediatric surgical specialists. Under "You and Your Family" its Web site provides safety information. There is a direct link to the State Highway Safety Organization Web site (www.statehighwaysafety.org) that lists child passenger safety state laws.

American Camping Association
5000 State Road 67 North
Martinsville, IN 46151-7902
Tel: (765) 342-8456
Fax: (765) 342-2065
www.acacamps.org

ACA is a community of camp professionals and is dedicated to enriching the lives of children and adults through the camp experience. Its Web site offers The Camp Knowledge Center, a comprehensive listing of resources in the 14 essential areas of camp management.

American Lung Association
1740 Broadway
New York, NY 10019
Tel: (212) 315-8700
(800) LUNG-USA or (800) 586-4872)
e-mail: info@lungusa.org
www..lungusa.org

The American Lung Association® (ALA) is the oldest voluntary health organization in the United States. Founded in 1904 to fight tuberculosis, ALA today fights lung disease in all its forms, with special emphasis on asthma, tobacco control and environmental health. Contributions from the public, along with gifts and grants from corporations, foundations and government agencies, fund ALA. ALA achieves its many successes through the work of thousands of committed volunteers and staff.

American Red Cross
2025 E Street, NW
Washington, DC 20006
Tel: (202) 728-6531
www.redcross.org

The American Red Cross, a humanitarian organization led by volunteers, guided by its Congressional Charter and the Fundamental Principles of the International Red Cross Movement, provides relief to victims of disasters and helps people prevent, prepare for, and respond to emergencies. Its Web site lists topical articles and devotes a section to Health and Safety.

American Society for Testing and Materials
100 Bar Harbor Drive
West Conshohocken, PA 19428-2959
Tel: (610) 832-9585
Fax: (610) 832-9555
www.astm.org

Organized in 1898, ASTM International is a not-for-profit organization that provides a forum for the development and publication of voluntary consensus standards for materials, products, systems and services. Playground equipment guidelines and standards; voluntary recommendations that aren't federally mandated or regulated are found on their Web site.

Autism Society of America
7910 Woodmont Avenue, Suite 300
Bethesda, MD 20814-3067
Tel: (301) 657-0881 or (800) 328-8476
Fax: (301) 657-0869
e-mail: info@autism-society.org
www.autism-society.org

ASA was founded in 1965 by a small group of parents working on a volunteer basis out of their homes. The society provides information and referral on autism. Its 20,000 members are connected through a working network of over 200 chapters in nearly every state. Its Web site has information packages that you may download.

Bicycle Helmet Safety Institute
4611 South 7th Street
Arlington, VA 22204-1419
Tel: (703) 486-0100 (and fax)
e-mail: info@helmets.org
www.bhsi.org

BHSI is a small, active non-profit that serves as a consumer advocacy program and a technical resource for bicycle helmet information. Its volunteers serve on the ASTM and ANSI bicycle helmet standard committees and are active in commenting on standards adopted by the Consumer Product Safety Commission. It's staffed by a few volunteers and funded entirely by consumer donations. Its extremely user-friendly Web site offers mandatory state and local helmet laws, a compendium of helmet and injury statistics, helmet standards, how to size a helmet.

Brain Injury Association
105 N. Alfred Street
Alexandria, VA 22314
Tel: (703) 236-6000
Fax: (703) 236-6001
www.biausa.org

The mission of the Brain Injury Association is to create a better future through brain injury prevention, research, education and advocacy. Its Web site provides .pdf and text versions of brochures *Brain Injury: The ABC Years,* and *Brain Injury: The Teenage Years,* printable fact sheets on injury statistics and prevention.

Child Welfare League of America, Inc.
440 1st Street, NW, 3rd Floor
Washington, DC 20001-2085
Tel: (202) 638-2952
Fax: (202) 638-4004
www.cwla.org

CWLA is an association of more than 1,100 public and private nonprofit agencies that assist over 3.5 million abused and neglected children and their families each year with a wide range of services.

Consumer Federation of America
1424 16th St., NW, Suite 604
Washington, DC 20036
Tel: (202) 387-6121
www.consumerfed.org

CFA is an advocacy organization, an educational organization and a membership organization of more than 285 organizations from throughout the nation with a combined membership exceeding 50 million people. Playground equipment guidelines and standards; voluntary recommendations that aren't federally mandated or regulated are found on this Web site.

Cooperative State Research, Education and Extension Service
U.S. Department of Agriculture
Washington, DC 20250-0900
Tel: (202) 720-3029
Fax: (202) 690-0289
e-mail: csrees@reeusda.gov
www.reeusda.gov

CSREES has research and education information about many subjects, and staff specialists who can answer your questions or refer you to someone at state or county level who possesses the information you need. Contact your local county extension office (offices are listed under local government in the telephone directory), a land-grant university or the Washington, D.C. headquarters.

Insurance Institute for Highway Safety
1005 N. Glebe Road, Suite 800
Arlington, VA 22201
Tel: (703) 247-1500
Fax: (703) 247-1588
www.iihs.org

For more than 30 years the IIHS has been a leader in finding out what works and doesn't work to prevent motor vehicle crashes in the first place and reduce injuries in the crashes that still occur. The Institute's affiliate organization, the Highway Loss Data Institute, gathers, processes, and publishes data on the ways in which insurance losses vary among different kinds of vehicles. Its Web site offers links to ratings for infant/toddler car seats.

National Alliance for the Mentally Ill
Colonial Place Three
2107 Wilson Boulevard, Suite 300
Arlington, VA 22201
Tel: (703) 524-7600
NAMI HelpLine: (800) 950-NAMI (6264)

NAMI is a nonprofit, grassroots, self-help, support and advocacy organization of consumers, families and friends of people with severe mental illnesses, such as schizophrenia, major depression, bipolar disorder, obsessive-compulsive disorder, and anxiety disorders. Its Web site gives information on illnesses and treatment.

National Alliance for Youth Sports
2050 Vista Parkway
West Palm Beach, FL 33411
Tel: (561) 684-1141; (800) 688-KIDS (5437)
Fax: (561) 684-2546
www.nays.org

NAYS is a nonprofit organization founded in 1981 to make sports safe and positive for America's youth. Programs educate volunteer coaches, parents, youth sport program administrations and officials about their roles and responsibilities in youth sports. They also offer youth development programs for children called Safe Start.

National Center for Bicycling and Walking
1394 Munger Street
Middlebury, VT 05753
Tel: (802) 388-2453
Fax: (802) 388-3288
www.bikefed.org

The Bicycle Federation of America, Inc., a national, nonprofit 501(c)(3) corporation established in 1977, works to create bicycle-friendly and walkable communities. To better call attention to its work on pedestrian- and bicycle-related issues, the BFA now operates as the National Center for Bicycling and Walking.

National Center for Injury Prevention & Control
4770 Buford Highway, NE
Atlanta, GA 30341-3727
Tel: (404) 488-4652
Fax: (404) 488-1317
e-mail: DUIPINFO@cdc.gov
www.cdc.gov/ncipc

The NCIPC publishes informative fact sheets on many of the topics discussed in this book.

National Center for Missing & Exploited Children
Charles B. Wang International Children's Building
699 Prince Street
Alexandria, VA 22314-3175
Tel: (703) 274-3900
Fax: (703) 274-2200
www.missingkids.org

NCMEC was created in 1984 as a public-private partnership and serves as the national clearinghouse for information on missing children and the prevention of child victimization. It works in partnership with the Office of Juvenile Justice and Delinquency Prevention of the Office of Justice Programs at the U.S. Department of Justice. The NCMEC Web site provides child protection information.

National Highway Traffic Safety Administration
Washington, DC
www.nhtsa.dot.gov

The NHTSA Web site offers recall information, safety resources and tips for injury prevention. The site also lists the agency's 10 regional offices and how to identify and contact the office serving your area.

National Institute of Mental Health
Public Inquiries
6001 Executive Boulevard, Room 8184, MSC 9663
Bethesda, MD 20892-9663
Tel: (301) 443-4513
Fax: (301) 443-4279
e-mail: nimhinfo@nih.gov
www.nimh.nih.gov
The "For Public" section of its Web site offers information from NIMH about the symptoms, diagnosis and treatment of mental illnesses. Included are brochures and information sheets, reports, press releases, fact sheets and other educational materials.

National Mental Health Association
1021 Prince Street
Alexandria, VA 22314
Tel: (800) 969-NMHA (6642)
TTY: (800) 433-5959
e-mail: infoctr@nmha.org
www.nmha.org

NMHA is the country's oldest and largest nonprofit organization addressing all aspects of mental health and mental illness. It works to improve the mental health of all Americans, through advocacy, education, research and service. Free fact sheets are available through its "Resource Center" on the association's Web site.

National Program for Playground Safety

School of Health, Physical Education & Leisure Services
WRC 205, University of Northern Iowa
Cedar Falls, IA 50614-0618
Tel: (800) 554-PLAY (7529)
Fax: (319) 273-7308
e-mail: playground-safety@uni.edu
www.uni.edu/playground

NPPS was established in 1995 through a grant from the Centers for Disease Control
and Prevention to address playground safety. It serves as a resource for the latest
information on playground safety and injury prevention. Look for safety tips,
Frequently Asked Questions and guides to playground inspection, supervision, design
and much more.

National SAFE KIDS Campaign

1301 Pennsylvania Avenue, NW, Suite 1000
Washington, DC 20004
Tel: (202) 662-0600
Fax: (202) 393-2072
www.safekids.org

The National SAFE KIDS Campaign is the only national organization dedicated solely
to the prevention of unintentional childhood injury — the number one killer of
children ages 14 and under. Former U.S. Surgeon General C. Everett Koop, M.D., Sc.D.,
is chairman of the Campaign. The organization's Web site offers statistics, fact sheets,
child protection laws listed by state, and information on preventive measures.

National Safety Council

1121 Spring Lake Drive
Itasca, IL 60143-3201
Tel: (630) 285-1121
Fax: (630) 285-1315
www.nsc.org

The National Safety Council, founded in 1913 and chartered by the United States
Congress in 1953, is the nation's leading advocate for safety and health. Its mission is
"to educate and influence society to adopt safety, health and environmental policies,
practices and procedures that prevent and mitigate human suffering and economic
losses arising from preventable causes."

National School Safety Center
4165 Thousand Oaks Boulevard, Suite 290
Westlake Village, CA 91362
Tel: (805) 373-9977
Fax: (805) 373-9277
e-mail: june@nssc1.org
www.jetlink.net/~nssc

The National School Safety Center was created by presidential directive in 1984 to meet the growing need for additional training and preparation in the area of school crime and violence prevention. Affiliated with Pepperdine University, NSSC is a nonprofit organization whose charge is to promote safe schools — free of crime and violence — and to help ensure quality education for all America's children.

Search Institute
700 S. Third Street, Suite 210
Minneapolis, MN 55415
Tel: (612) 376-8955; (800) 888-7828
Fax: (612) 376-8956
e-mail: si@search-institute.org
www.search-institute.org
Organizations wanting to be proactive about drugs and alcohol abuse might want to contact the Search Institute in Minneapolis, Minn., which provides positive youth development strategies. The Institute was founded in 1958 as an applied social science research organization focused on the healthy development of young people. This mission has evolved to advance the well-being of adolescents and children by generating knowledge and promoting its application. At the heart of the Institute's work is the framework of 40 developmental assets, which are positive experiences, relationships, opportunities, and personal qualities that young people need to grow up healthy, caring, and responsible.

Underwriters Laboratory
www.ul.com

Underwriters Laboratories Inc. is an independent, not-for-profit product safety testing and certification organization. UL has tested products for public safety for more than a century. Each year, more than 16 billion UL Marks are applied to products worldwide. Contact UL through the organization's Web site, which offers e-mail forms for inquiries.

U.S. Consumer Product Safety Commission
Office of Information and Public Affairs
Washington, DC 20207
4330 East-West Highway
Bethesda, MD 20814-4408
Tel: (301) 504-0990
Fax: (301) 504-0124 and (301) 504-0025
e-mail: info@cpsc.gov
www.cpsc.gov

Toll-free consumer hotline: *800-638-2772 (TTY 800-638-8270). Call to obtain product safety information and other agency information and to report unsafe products. Available 24 hours a day, 7 days a week.*

The CPSC Web site has a "Special 4Kids" section with printable tips designed for kids' own safety, Frequently Asked Questions, Publications and National Injury Information Clearinghouse. The site also features playground equipment guidelines and standards; and voluntary recommendations that aren't federally mandated or regulated.

U.S. Fire Administration, The
Office of Fire Management Programs
16825 S. Seton Avenue
Emmitsburg, MD 21727
Tel: (301) 447-1000
Fax: (301) 447-1052
www.firesafety.com

The United States Fire Administration, a directorate within the Federal Emergency Management Agency, is the national leader in fire safety and prevention, supporting the efforts of local communities to reduce the number of fires and fire deaths.

U.S. Lifesaving Association, The
P.O. Box 366
Huntington Beach, CA 92648
(866) FOR-USLA
www.usla.org

Public education, national lifeguard standards, training programs to reduce death and injury in aquatic environments and related information are available on this organization's informative Web site.

Legislation

Many laws may be found on the Cornell University's Legal Information Institute Web site, www.law.cornell.edu. This site can be searched by topic to locate applicable federal and state laws. It also lists standards for products such as cribs; bunk beds; rattles; bicycle helmets; swimming pool slides; and flammability of children's sleepwear, or carpets and rugs, or mattresses and mattress pads.

Child-resistant closures
- The Child Protection Act of 1966, www.cpsc.gov/CPSCPUB/PUBS/282.html
- Poison Prevention Packaging Act of 1970, www.mindspring.com/~methinfex/filecab/cfr/16cfr1700.pdf

Choking hazard warning labels
■ The Child Safety Protection Act

Guns
■ Gun Free Schools Act of 1994

Inappropriate for use by children
■ Labeling of Hazardous Art Materials Act of 1988 www.cpsc.gov/cpscpub/pubs/5016.html

Internet
■ Children's Online Privacy Protection Act of 1998. For key provisions of the Final Rule applying to COPPA, visit: http://www.ftc.gov/opa/1999/9910/childfinal.htm

Poison treatment
■ Poison Control Center Enhancement and Awareness Act of 2000

Reduce childhood lead poisoning
■ The Lead-Based Paint Prevention Act of 1971
■ Residential Lead-Based Paint Hazard Reduction Act of 1992

Regulate public playgrounds
■ Safe Playgrounds Act of 2001 (H. R. 2159) Provides grants to states to enact statewide laws consistent with playground safety guidelines established by the Consumer Product Safety Commission. thomas.loc.gov/

Standards

Bicycle Helmets, Drawstrings on Children's Clothing
■ U.S. Consumer Product Safety Commission Safety Standards 1999

Child restraint devices
■ Federal Motor Vehicle Standard 213 (FMVSS 213).

Child-resistant disposable and novelty cigarette lighters
■ U.S. Consumer Product Safety Commission Mandatory Safety Standard, 1994

Public playground safety
■ Handbook for Public Playground Safety, Playground Safety Guidelines, CPSC

Voluntary Toy Safety Standards
■ Standard Consumer Safety Specification of Toy Safety (ASTM F963

Toy Firearms
■ U.S. Department of Commerce "Marking of Toy Look-Alike and Imitation Firearms" regulation

Bibliography

Books

A Parent's Guide to Preventing Inhalant Abuse, National Inhalant Abuse Prevention Center, Washington, D.C., 1998.

Besherov, Douglas, *Recognizing Child Abuse: A Guide for the Concerned*, Free Press, New York, N.Y., 1990.

Carnegie Council on Adolescent Development, Task Force on Youth Development and Community Programs, *A Matter of Time: Risk and Opportunity in the Nonschool Hours*, Carnegie Corp., New York, N.Y., 1992.

Consumer Product Safety Commission Staff, *Safety Hazards in Child Care Settings*, U.S. Consumer Product Safety Commission, Washington, D.C., April 1999.

Davin, Patricia, Teresa Dunbar and Julia Hislop, *Female Sexual Abusers: Three Views*, The Safer Society Foundation, Brandon, Vt., 1999.

Donnelley, Anne Cohn, *An Approach to Preventing Child Abuse*, National Committee to Prevent Child Abuse, Chicago, Ill., 1983.

Flannery, Daniel J, *School Violence: Risk, Preventive Intervention and Policy*, Columbia University, New York, N.Y., 1997.

Garbarino, James, *Lost Boys: Why Our Sons Turn Violent and How We Can Save Them*, Free Press, New York, N.Y., 1999.

Garbarino, James and A. C. Garbarino, *Emotional Maltreatment of Children*, National Committee to Prevent Child Abuse, Inc., Chicago, Ill., 1986.

Garner, Bryan A. (Editor), *Black's Law Dictionary*, 7th edition, West Group, Eagan, Minn., 1999.

Green, Morris (Editor), *Bright Futures: Guidelines for Health Supervision of Infants, Children and Adolescents,* National Center for Education in Maternal and Child Health, Arlington, Va., 1994.

Herman, Melanie, *Full Speed Ahead: Managing Technology Risk in the Nonprofit World,* Nonprofit Risk Management Center, Washington, D.C., 2001.

Jackson, Peggy M., Leslie T. White and Melanie L. Herman, *Mission Accomplished: A Practical Guide to Risk Management for Nonprofits (2nd Edition),* Nonprofit Risk Management Center, Washington, D.C., 1999.

Jones, Lisa and David Finkelhor, *The Decline in Sexual Abuse Cases,* Office of Juvenile Justice and Delinquency Prevention, Washington, D.C., 2001.

Mind Over Matter: The Brain's Response to Drugs. "Teachers' Guide," National Clearinghouse for Alcohol and Drug Information, National Institutes of Health, Rockville, Md., 1997.

Monteleone, J. A., *Recognition of Child Abuse for the Mandated Reporter,* G.W. Medical Publishing, St. Louis, Mo., 1994.

National Collaboration for Youth, *Screening Volunteers to Prevent Child Sexual Abuse: A Community Guide for Youth Organizations,* National Assembly of National Voluntary Health and Social Welfare Organizations, Washington, D.C., 1997.

National Research Council, *Understanding Child Abuse and Neglect,* National Academy Press, Washington, D.C., 1993.

Patterson, John, *Staff Screening Tool Kit: Building a Strong Foundation Through Careful Staffing (2nd Edition),* Nonprofit Risk Management Center, Washington, D.C., 1998.

Research on Children and Adolescents with Mental, Behavioral and Developmental Disorders: Mobilizing a National Initiative, Institute of Medicine, National Academy of Sciences Press, Washington, D.C., 1989.

Ryan, Gail and Sandy Lane, editors, *Juvenile Sexual Offending: Causes, Consequences and Correction,* Lexington Books, Lexington, Mass., 1991.

Singer, M., D. Miller, K. Slovak and R. Frierson, *Mental health consequences of children's exposure to violence,* Case Western Reserve University, Mandel School of Applied Social Sciences, Cleveland, Ohio, 1997.

Sobsey, Dick, *Violence and abuse in the lives of people with disabilities: the end of silent acceptance,* Paul H. Brooks Publishing, Baltimore, Md., 1994.

Widome, Mark D. (Editor), *Injury Prevention and Control for Children and Youth,* Committee on Injury and Poison Prevention, American Academy of Pediatrics, Elk Grove Village, Ill., 1997.

Articles from Reports, Magazines, Newsletters and Online Publications

"2 Estimation Methodology for Children with a Serious Emotional Disturbance," *Federal Register,* Oct. 6, 1997, pgs. 52139-52144.

"Baseball Safety Factsheet," Document #329, pg. 1, Consumer Product Safety Commission, Washington, D.C.

"Be Alert to Signs of Carbon Monoxide Poisoning," Underwriter's Laboratory, www.ul.com/consumers/

Becker, Judith, "Offenders: Characteristics and Treatment," *The Future of Children: Sexual Abuse of Children,* Vol. 4, No. 2, 1994, pgs. 176-197, The David and Lucille Packard Foundation, Los Angeles, Calif.

"Bicycle Safety," fact sheet, Brain Injury Association, Alexandria, Va., April 2001, www.biausa.org.

"Bullies: A Serious Problem for Kids," National Crime Prevention Council, Washington, D.C.

"Carbon Monoxide (CO)" fact sheet, Environmental Protection Agency, Washington, D.C., www.epa.gov/iaq.

"Child Passenger Safety Fact Sheet," National Center for Injury Prevention and Control, Washington, D.C., Nov. 13, 2000, www.cdc.gov/ncipc.

Cloud, John, "Out, Proud and Very Young," *Time,* Dec. 8, 1997, Vol. 150, No. 24.

Cox News Service, "Teen Survey Finds High Risk Activities," *San Francisco Chronicle,* Aug. 14, 1998, page A-8.

"CPSC Learns of More Injuries, Teachers Should Not Let Children Move or Play Near TV or Audiovisual Carts," Consumer Product Safety Commission, Document #5102.

"Drowning Prevention," fact sheet, National Center for Injury Prevention and Control, Washington, D.C., Oct. 27, 2000, www.cdc.gov/ncipc.

"Equipment Maintenance Guidelines for Playgrounds," National Program for Playground Safety, Cedar Falls, Iowa, www.uni.edu/playground.

"Exposing an Invisible Killer: The Dangers of Carbon Monoxide," U.S. Fire Administration, Office of Fire Management Programs, Emmitsburg, Md., Dec. 17, 2001.

"Facts on Adolescent Injury" fact sheet, National Center for Injury Prevention and Control, Washington, D.C., July 2, 1999, www.cdc.gov/ncipc.

"Fact Sheet: Carbon Monoxide," American Lung Association, New York, N.Y., September 2000.

"Fact Sheet: Suicide," American Academy of Pediatrics, Elk Grove Village, Ill., 1999.

"Falls," fact sheet, Brain Injury Association, Alexandria, Va., March 2001, www.viausa.org.

"Fatality Facts: Teenagers as of October 2000," Insurance Institute for Highway Safety, Highway Loss Data Institute, Arlington, Va., Feb. 6, 2001, www.hwysafety.org.

"Fatality Facts: Children as of October 2000," Insurance Institute for Highway Safety, Highway Loss Data Institute, Arlington, Va., Feb. 6, 2001, www.hwysafety.org.

"Fireworks-Related Injuries," fact sheet, National Center for Injury Prevention and Control, Washington, D.C., June 15, 2001, www.cdc.gov/ncipc.

"Household and Family Characteristics: March 1998 (Update)," pgs. 20-515, *Current Population Reports*, U.S. Bureau of the Census, and earlier reports.

Howell, James C., "Youth Gangs: an Overview," *Juvenile Justice Bulletin*, August 1988, Office of Juvenile Justice and Delinquency Prevention, U.S. Department of Justice, Washington, D.C.

Huff, C. Ronald, "Comparing the Criminal Behavior of Youth Gangs and At-Risk Youths," *Research in Brief*, October 1988, National Institute of Justice, U.S. Department of Justice, Washington, D.C.

"IAQ Fact Sheet: Carbon Monoxide" fact sheet, Environmental Health Center, A Division of the National Safety Council, Washington, D.C., www.nsc.org.

"Injury Facts: Airway Obstruction," National SAFE KIDS Campaign, www.safekids.org.

"Injury Facts: Bike Injury," National SAFE KIDS Campaign, www.safekids.org.

"Injury Facts: Childhood Injury," National SAFE KIDS Campaign, www.safekids.org.

"Injury Facts: Children at Risk," National SAFE KIDS Campaign, www.safekids.org.

"Injury Facts: Drowning," National SAFE KIDS Campaign, www.safekids.org.

"Injury Facts: Falls," National SAFE KIDS Campaign, www.safekids.org.

"Injury Facts: Pedestrian Injury," National SAFE KIDS Campaign, www.safekids.org.

"Injury Facts: Motor Vehicle Occupant," National SAFE KIDS Campaign, www.safekids.org.

"Injury Facts: Playground Injury," National SAFE KIDS Campaign, www.safekids.org.

"Injury Facts: Poisoning," National SAFE KIDS Campaign, www.safekids.org.

"Injury Facts: School Injuries," National SAFE KIDS Campaign, www.safekids.org.

"Injury Facts: Sports and Recreational Activity Injury," National SAFE KIDS Campaign, www.safekids.org.

"Injury Facts: Toy Injury," National SAFE KIDS Campaign, www.safekids.org.

Lenaway, D.D., A.G. Ambler and D.E. Beaudoin, "The epidemiology of school-related injuries: new perspectives," *American Journal of Preventive Medicine*, Vol. 8, 1992, pgs. 193-198.

Lotke, Eric and Vincent Schiraldi, "An Analysis of Juvenile Homicides: Where They Occur and the Effectiveness of Adult Court Intervention," National Center on Institutions and Alternatives, Washington, D.C.

"Motor Vehicle-Related Crashes Among Teenagers," fact sheet, National Center for Injury Prevention and Control, Washington, D.C., April 7, 2000, www.cdc.gov/ncipc.

"Normal Adolescent Development," Center for Adolescent Studies, University of Indiana, Bloomington, Ind. 1997. See http://education.indiana.edu/cas/adol/development.html.

OJJDP Juvenile Justice Bulletin, October 2001, U.S. Department of Justice, Office of Justice Programs, Office of Juvenile Justice and Delinquency Prevention, pg. 1.

Papazian, Ruth, "Women and Boys — Sexual Assault or Initiation? The Law Says Rape, but Americans Are Ambivalent," March 30, 2000, www.apbnews.com.

"Playground Injuries" fact sheet, National Center for Injury Prevention and Control, Washington, D.C., Jan. 27, 2000, www.cdc.gov/ncipc.

"Playground Inspection Guide: 10 Steps to Safer Playgrounds for Children," National Program for Playground Safety, Cedar Falls, Iowa, www.uni.edu/playground.

"Policy Statement: Trampolines at Home, School and Recreational Centers, " American Academy of Pediatrics, pg. 1, www.aap.org/policy/re9844.html.

"Preventing Bicycle-related Head Injuries" fact sheet, National Center for Injury Prevention and Control, Washington, D.C., Jan. 27, 2000, www.cdc.gov/ncipc.

"Public Playground Checklist," Playground Buddies, 4Kids, U.S. Consumer Product Safety Commission, www.cpsc.gov.

Randolph, Norman, Alan McEvoy and Edsel Erickson, "Why the Brutality?", *Youth Gangs: Guidelines for Educators and Community Youth Leaders*, Learning Publications, Holmes Beach, Fla., 1998. Posted on the Urban Education Web site http://eric-web.tc.columbia.edu/administration/safety/gang_brutality/index.html.

"Safety Links," National SAFE KIDS Campaign, www.safekids.org.

"Scooter Safety," fact sheet, Brain Injury Association, Alexandria, Va., March 2001, www.biausa.org.

Stephens, Ronald D., "School-Based Interventions: Safety and Security," pages 221-223, *The Gang Intervention Handbook,* Research Press, Champaign, Ill., 1993.

"Supervision Guidelines for Playgrounds," National Program for Playground Safety, Cedar Falls, Iowa, www.uni.edu/playground.

"Timely Topics/Soccer," www.toledoacadmed.org/TimelyTopics/soccer.html.

"Unintentional Injury Fact Sheet on Childhood Injury," National Center for Injury Prevention and Control, Centers for Disease Control, Washington, D.C., www.cdc.gov/ncipc/duip/childh.htm.

Violence Prevention: A Vision of Hope, California Attorney General's Office, Crime and Youth Prevention Center, Sacramento, Calif., 1995.

"You Don't Need to be Knocked Out to Have a Concussion," The Pashby Sport Concussion Safety Web site, www.concussionsafety.com/concussion.

"Youth Risk Behavior Surveillance — United States 1993," *Morbidity and Mortality Weekly Report*, Vol. 44, No. SS-1, 1995, pg. 47, Centers for Disease Control, U.S. Department of Health and Human Services, Washington, D.C.

"Youth Risk Behavior Surveillance — United States 1997," *Morbidity and Mortality Weekly Report,* Centers for Disease Control, 1998.